"When I was in junior high, my mom traveled internationally. Whenever she returned, we just had to try to re-create in our home the wonderful dishes she'd encountered all over the world. Luckily for us, we lived in New York City, where we could find every ingredient we needed, and more, in Hell's Kitchen (which should have been called Heaven's Kitchen, as far as we were concerned). A generation later, at a moment when acre after acre of the city's earthiness is being bulldozed in favor of hulking glass towers, Hell's Kitchen has somehow survived intact.

"Carliss's book—her recipes, stories, and photos—captures the neighborhood's legendary flavor and funk between two covers. *Sizzle* is not only good eating and good reading, it is an act of heartening urban conservation."

—Sara Moulton, host of *Sara's Weeknight Meals* on Public Television; executive chef, *Gourmet* magazine; and food editor, *Good Morning America.*

sizzle

ethnic recipes from restaurants of

in hell's

New York City's Ninth Avenue neighborhood

kitchen

Carliss Retif Pond

GIBBS SMITH
TO ENRICH AND INSPIRE HUMANKIND
Salt Lake City | Charleston | Santa Fe | Santa Barbara

First Edition
1 2 3 4 5   09 10 11 12 13

To The People of Hell's Kitchen
Past, Present and Future

In memory of Daddy, Mama, Grandaddy
and Polly, with much love and gratitude

Text © 2009 by Carliss Retif Pond
Photographs on pages 40, 41, 42, 43, 66, 67,
69, 86, 88, 89, 110, 111, 130, 154, 155, 172, 215
© 2009 by Andy Hoets.
Photograph on page 132 © 2009 by Carliss Retif Pond.
All other photographs from Shutterstock.com.

Published by
Gibbs Smith
P.O. Box 667
Layton, Utah 84041

Orders: 1.800.835.4993
www.gibbs-smith.com

Designed by Debra McQuiston
Printed and bound in China

Library of Congress Cataloging-in-Publication Data

Pond, Carliss Retif.
Sizzle in Hell's Kitchen : ethnic recipes from
restaurants of New York City's
Ninth Avenue neighborhood / Carliss Retif Pond.
— 1st ed.
p. cm.
ISBN-13: 978-1-4236-0445-7
ISBN-10: 1-4236-0445-8
1. Cookery, International. 2. Hell's Kitchen (New
York, N.Y.) I. Title.
TX725.A1P645 2009
641.59—dc22
2008042799

The concept of this book was mine but the realization of it would never have been if not for the love and support of friends and family and the amazing talent and professionalism of so many individuals, too numerous to name.

Very special thanks to:

Guillermo Vidal, who first introduced me to the delightful world of Hell's Kitchen and its people. Our meeting was a turning point in my life.

Maria Decaney, my invaluable assistant and dear friend, whose talent, dedication and expertise is unparalleled. And to darling Max, who never complained about time spent away from him.

George Anderson, an HK resident who encouraged me from beginning to end and constantly, through wit and logic, put things in perspective whenever I lost focus.

Barbara Pope, my longtime friend and confidant in Philadelphia, who found the correct words when all had escaped me.

Madge Baird, my editor, who patiently guided me through the process of writing this book.

Gibbs Smith, my publisher, for his belief in the book concept.

Mother, who has always disliked the kitchen and cooking but is one of the best cooks I know.

All the restaurateurs, chefs, cooks, workers, proprietors and residents who gave so generously of their time and information.

CONTENTS

Said one famous actor, "I come to the neighborhood to eat because I'm safe here. No one cares who you are or what you do—everyone's the same."

When I moved to Manhattan a decade ago, I had heard of a great food shopping and eating area—Ninth Avenue. Unsure as to what to expect but being a devoted foodie, I set out to discover what all the talk was about. Surely, it couldn't possibly compare to the marketplaces and restaurants in Paris, Rome, Cairo and other great food centers, could it?

My adventure began early in the day as I set out to explore the myriad shops and eating establishments. My initial skepticism evaporated immediately when I discovered that I was in a microcosm of the world. Not only were there French, Italian and Mediterranean cuisines and cultures, but also Ethiopian, Russian, Thai, Iraqi, Druze, German and more. I felt overwhelmed, in a good way, with the variety and abundance of international culinary products.

As I spoke with neighborhood merchants and residents, I was delighted to learn that I was in the middle of Hell's Kitchen, a place known around the world through movies, television, theater and books. Emphasis had always been put on the area's colorful history and characters but little on its ethnically diverse foods. My leisurely shopping day initiated an insatiable appetite to not only indulge in the eating experience but also capture the recipes, traditions and stories. So, on Ash Wednesday 2001, the concept for this book was born. I had no idea where the road would lead but I was ready for the journey. And what a wonderful journey it has been!

Before I delved into the recipes and resident conversations, I had to know the basics. Hell's Kitchen could not be limited to Ninth Avenue, so how much territory did it cover and what were the boundaries? Also, how in the world could a neighborhood come to be known as Hell's Kitchen? As I began my research, my first surprise came with the puzzled looks on the faces of those living and working here. Their question was always the same: "Why do you want to know these things? We're born here, work here and die here. It's simple." That's when I realized they take the magnitude of this treasure for granted. Yes, they love it and stay generation after generation. They know it is special to them but don't assume it would be special to anyone else.

While there are no distinct boundaries, Hell's Kitchen is considered to lie between West 34th and West 57th Streets and from Eighth Avenue to the Hudson River. On the eastern boundary, the neighborhood overlaps the Times Square theater district. On the southeast side, it overlaps the Garment District; on the northern edge, Hell's Kitchen is two blocks south of Central Park and on the western edge is the Hudson River.

In the seventeenth century, this area was known as Bloemendael and was an idyllic Dutch setting with landed gentry. While there are different versions as to how it became Hell's Kitchen, the most common anecdote goes back to the late 1800s. A veteran policeman, Dutch Fred the Cop, and his rookie partner watched a violent brawl on West 39th Street between Ninth and Tenth Avenues. Shocked, the rookie exclaimed, "This is Hell!" to which Fred matter-of-factly responded, "Hell is cool compared to this. This is Hell's kitchen!" The name remains, although it is sometimes referred to as Clinton or Midtown West.

At that time in Hell's Kitchen history, Ninth Avenue became a flourishing pushcart marketplace known as Paddy's Market. Droves of people came from all over Manhattan to shop in open-air markets for spices, oils, breads, fish, poultry, meats and produce. The stage was set, and today this immigrant neighborhood continues to be one of New York City's major food venues for chefs, home cooks, restaurant-goers and anyone who loves to eat.

A walk in the area offers innumerable ethnic food shops and restaurants. Both locals and tourists flock to the neighborhood, assured that a rare, indispensable ingredient or a favorite dish will be found—perhaps a special butcher cut black pepper, or oxtails, or a special tapa from Spain or a delectable brandade from France!

Many people shop the day away and then slip inside a restaurant for dinner in the country of their choice. Surrounded by authentic cultural decor, diners are transported, reliving childhood or favorite travel memories. How often I've heard, "This avgolemono is exactly the way my Greek grandmother made it . . . This doro wat reminds me of that Ethiopian village . . . That Italian villa—the bagna cauda—delicioso!" Tastes, aromas and reminiscences!

Blessed with generations of ethnic diversity, strong community and a cornucopia of food and drink, Hell's Kitchen has also been blessed with location. Because it overlaps New York's Theater District, HK restaurants are packed with avid theatergoers both before and after the shows. When I asked Lidia Bastianich why she chose this site for Becco's, she responded, "I wanted to serve customers the freshest ingredients in delicious dishes while still getting them to the show on time." Oftentimes, theatergoers are so involved in their eating adventure that they are unaware of Broadway actors and celebrities at the table next to them. One famous actor told me, "I come to the neighborhood because I'm safe here. No one cares who you are or what you do—everyone's the same." A perfect summation of the nature of the area—especially with so many different cultures.

Writing a cookbook entails collecting recipes, testing them and, of course, eating everything "to make sure," the latter being the most envious part of the process! What is sometimes forgotten are the people—and their sto-ries—who give life to the food and recipes. For years, I've lived in the neigh-borhood, shopping, eating, chatting on stoops in the evenings, and I thought I knew everyone. But it was only when I asked them to go back as far as they could remember that the deluge came:

Bobby Esposito's grandfather founded Giovanni Esposito & Sons Meat Shop (38th Street and Ninth Avenue) when he arrived from Naples in the 1920s. He raised ten children across the street from the business. Today in the same location, his grandson Bobby still supplies thousands of pounds of sausage weekly to individuals and city restaurants.

Upon seeing the Hudson River when arriving from Greece, Andy Fable's grandfather decided to open his Poseidon "god of the sea" Bakery. With the bakery on the ground floor, the family lived upstairs to combine family and business. The tradition continues today. As Andy's wife, Lillian, says, "We're keeping up the tradition. We're the last Manhattan shop to make phyllo by hand. We can run downstairs at 5:00 a.m., start flouring the boards and roll-ing the baklava without leaving home." Lily and Andy's son Paul (the fourth generation) can be found every day in the shop preparing delectable Greek specialties. Good news: people line up to buy their light phyllo delicacies. Bad news: all recipes are family secrets.

When I asked ninety-year-old Camilla Pollio what she remembered most about growing up in Hell's Kitchen, she looked perplexed. Too general! My question switched to, "When you were ten?" Her eyes sparkled. "My father worked at the Runkel's Chocolate Factory and he came home every night with cocoa packed in his hair. My mother scrubbed the pillowcases on a washboard. I almost forgot!"

Today, Paul Vaccari and his brother Peter are carrying on the family's retail meat business at Piccinini Brothers. Their grandfather and his half-brother

Mauro Piccinini established the shop in 1922. The shop—with one of the city's first walk-in freezers, marble counters and sawdust floors—was as colorful as its clientele. The mix included speakeasies and restaurants as well as housewives and actors like Jimmy Durante and Walter Matthau. When Paul reminisces, he smiles and says, "My grandmother worked here until she died at 104."

A tiny seafood store, DeMartino's might be passed by, but it has been supplying the neighborhood and restaurants for almost a century. Eighty-year-old Joe could be found dozing in his chair every day in the shop, but a slight nudge would get him up smiling and placing your order into a brown paper bag. I was lucky to have sat and chatted with him before his death in December 2007. As he went back in time, he recollected, "When I was twelve, my brother and I would go to the store after school. My father cleaned the seafood, my mother boxed it, and we delivered it." The business is still in the family and remains a neighborhood fixture.

The stories about life in the neighborhood are as abundant and diverse as the people and their food. It would be impossible to tell all of them, or it would need its own book. Here, I can only hope to capture the essence of the people and their foods through the remembrances expressed above.

Finally, I am constantly being asked what my favorite dish is, my favorite restaurant. I have always found those questions to be curious, as I cannot imagine choosing one of anything. It's cliché but true, "Variety is the spice of life"—so why not go for it! And that's what Hell's Kitchen offers. Locals and tourists alike can "travel" to various countries to indulge in whatever ethnic feast they crave on any particular day. And the best part: it's all within walking distance. Whether you live here or are here for a visit, you're sure to find what you're craving, and perhaps a slice of heaven!

Soups of

Beer
Cheese

or

Cream of
Potato

A veteran policeman, Dutch Fred the Cop, and his rookie partner watched a violent brawl on West 39th Street between Ninth and Tenth Avenues. Shocked, the rookie exclaimed, "This is Hell!" to which Fred matter-of-factly responded, "Hell is cool compared to this. This is Hell's kitchen!"

bacon-wrapped dates

Cafe Andalucia, Spanish Tapas, courtesy of Guillermo Vidal

The crunchiness and contrast of sweet and salty make this Spanish tapas dish a real crowd pleaser. They will go quickly, so make sure there are many available. More good news is they can be made ahead and refrigerated. Pecans or walnuts can be substituted for the almonds.

SERVES 6 (30 PIECES)

30 (about 1/2 pound) pitted dates
30 whole almonds
30 bacon strips*
Mixed greens
Assorted olives for garnish

1 Stuff each date with an almond.

2 Roll each date tightly in 1 strip bacon.

3 In batches, place in a large heavy skillet over high heat. Cook on one side 5 to 6 minutes, pressing down with a spatula, until bacon is browned and crisp.

4 Turn dates over, lower heat and cook 3 to 4 minutes, until bacon is crispy.

5 Serve on a bed of mixed greens with olives.

* Turkey bacon can be substituted.

blackened sea scallops with creole mustard sauce

Delta Grill, Louisiana Cuisine, courtesy of Ignacio Castillo

Sea scallops are larger than bay scallops and are sometimes sold as "diver" scallops. When purchasing, look for a firm, not melting, texture.

SERVES 4
SEASONING MIX MAKES 2³/₄ CUPS

SCALLOPS
8 large sea scallops
1¹/₂ tablespoons Delta Grill Cajun Seasoning mix
3 tablespoons olive oil

DELTA GRILL CAJUN SAUCE
1 tablespoon butter
¹/₂ cup Creole mustard (or other coarse-grain mustard)
¹/₄ cup heavy cream
¹/₄ cup chicken stock
1¹/₂ teaspoons Delta Grill Cajun Seasoning

GARNISH
Flat-leaf parsley, chopped

DELTA GRILL CAJUN SEASONING MIX
¹/₂ cup salt
4 tablespoons white pepper
4 tablespoons garlic powder
4 tablespoons onion powder
2 tablespoons cumin
2 tablespoons mustard powder
³/₄ cup Spanish paprika
4 tablespoons ground black pepper
2 tablespoons chili powder
¹/₂ teaspoon cayenne
2 tablespoons dried thyme
2 tablespoons dried basil
2 tablespoons dried oregano

SCALLOPS
1 Preheat oven to 400 degrees F.

2 Season scallops with seasoning mix. Coat well with olive oil.

3 Heat a large oven-ready skillet on high heat.

4 Add scallops and sauté 30 seconds on each side, until a light brown crust forms. Remove from heat and place in the oven for 3 minutes.

5 Remove from oven, tent with foil and keep warm.

DELTA GRILL CAJUN SAUCE
6 In a clean skillet, melt butter.

7 Add mustard, heavy cream, stock and seasoning.

8 Blend all ingredients and simmer until thickened.

9 Plate 2 scallops per person and top with sauce.

10 Garnish with chopped parsley.

DELTA GRILL CAJUN SEASONING MIX
11 Thoroughly combine all ingredients.

NOTE: Can be stored in an airtight jar. Recipe can be halved.

seared marinated quail with orzo risotto

Le Madeleine, Modern French, courtesy of Fabian Pauta

Also known as bobwhites, these tiny birds are tender and succulent and make an elegant first course. Italian for "barley," orzo may look like rice but is actually a semolina pasta.

SERVES 4

MARINADE
1/2 white onion
2 cloves garlic
1/2 cup soy sauce
1/2 cup olive oil
2 quail, 4 to 5 ounces each, semi-boned and halved

ORZO RISOTTO
1/2 white onion, cut in small dice
1 clove garlic, chopped
1 cup orzo pasta
1/4 cup white wine
1/4 cup heavy cream
2 cups chicken stock
1 tablespoon butter
Salt and pepper to taste

GARNISH
Frisée

MARINADE

1 In a blender, puree onion, garlic, soy sauce and olive oil.

2 Place quail in a shallow baking pan. Cover with marinade and let marinate for 2 hours in the refrigerator.

ORZO RISOTTO

3 In a heavy saucepan, sauté onions and garlic for 2 minutes until soft. (Do not brown).

4 Add the orzo and sauté for 1 minute.

5 Over medium heat, whisk in wine and cream, and cook until slightly thickened.

6 Add the chicken stock, 1/2 cup at a time, until the pasta is cooked.

7 Whisk in butter and salt and pepper to taste.

TO COMPLETE THE DISH

8 Sear quail in a hot pan until crispy, about 2 minutes on each side.

9 On individual plates, place 3 tablespoons of the Orzo Risotto.

10 Top with a quail and season with salt and pepper. Garnish with frisée.

salt cod brandade

Marseille, South of France, courtesy of Peter Larsen

This ancient dish from the South of France is also popular in Spain and Portugal. When a fisherman's catch was abundant, there was a need to preserve. The cod was salt cured and sun dried for future use. Therefore, the soaking step in this recipe is necessary to remove all excess salt.

SERVES 4

1/2 pound salt cod
Water
2 cups heavy cream
1 clove garlic, thinly sliced
1 small baking, or russet, potato (baked in foil at 350 degrees F until tender), peeled
1/3 teaspoon grated nutmeg
1/2 cup milk
1/3 cup extra virgin olive oil plus oil to drizzle
Salt (Maldon or Fleur de Sel)
Croutons, toasted baguette, crudités

1 Soak cod in a large bowl of water to cover by 1 inch, refrigerated, for 2 days. Change water twice daily to remove excess salt.

2 Drain cod well and pat dry.

3 Poach cod in cream with garlic for 15 minutes.

4 Strain and reserve garlic.

5 In a food processor, combine cod, reserved garlic, peeled potato, and nutmeg. Process while gradually adding milk and olive oil until smooth.

6 Divide cod among four individual ramekins.

7 Bake in preheated 350-degree-F oven for 5 minutes.

8 Place under broiler until golden brown.

9 Drizzle with olive oil and sprinkle with salt.

10 Serve with croutons, toasted baguette slices or crudités.

hommus tahini

La Kabbr, Middle Eastern, courtesy of Farouk Mansoor

A classic for centuries throughout the Middle East, hommus is now a favorite dish around the world. This protein-rich appetizer can be served with pita and/or crudités.

YIELDS ABOUT 2 CUPS

2 cups cooked chickpeas
3 cloves garlic, minced
1/2 cup tahini (sesame paste)
1–2 tablespoons fresh lemon juice (more or less to taste)
Olive oil to drizzle

1 If using dried chickpeas, cook according to package directions.

2 If using canned chickpeas, drain, rinse and dry.

3 Place chickpeas, garlic, tahini and lemon juice in a food processor and process until smooth and creamy.

4 Place in a serving bowl, drizzle with olive oil and serve at room temperature.

seared white tuna with garlic sauce

Bamboo 52, Japanese, courtesy of Kevin Wunkei Chan

The small blowtorch used to sear the tuna in this recipe is available in hardware and cookware stores. It is widely used in browning the surface of the French dessert crème brûlée.

SERVES 4

GARLIC SAUCE
4 cloves garlic, minced
3 tablespoons water
1 tablespoon soy sauce
1 tablespoon mirin (Japanese sweet cooking wine)
1 tablespoon regular sake
$1/2$ red onion, chopped
$1/4$ teaspoon freshly grated ginger

TUNA
$1/2$ pound white tuna
Shichimi (Japanese 7-spice blend)

GARLIC SAUCE

1. In a sauté pan, bring all sauce ingredients to a boil and thicken 2 to 3 minutes, stirring constantly.

2 Remove from heat and keep warm.

TUNA

3 Sprinkle tuna with shichimi.

4 With a small blowtorch, sear both surfaces of the tuna.

5 Dice the tuna into $1/2$-inch cubes and drizzle with garlic sauce.

ALTERNATE METHOD

6 If a blowtorch is not available, heat a large skillet over high heat and brush with olive oil.

7 Add tuna and sear 30 seconds on each side, being careful not to cook interior.

8 Proceed with above preparation.

apple cider–braised pork belly with cranberry chutney and apple frisée salad

West Bank Cafe, Progressive American, courtesy of Joe Marcus

Pork belly is just another name for a slab of unsmoked bacon. It is made more succulent and moist when braised in apple cider. Served on a swirl of celery root puree and Cranberry Chutney and with Apple Frisée Salad, this rustic dish is reminiscent of a French countryside dinner.

SERVES 4-6

PORK
$1/2$ cup canola oil
1 (3-pound) pork belly

2 stalks celery, chopped
1 small onion, chopped
1 small carrot, chopped
3 cloves garlic, chopped
2 bay leaves
1 tablespoon black peppercorns

$1/2$ cup red wine
2 cups chicken stock
2 cups apple cider
1 cup veal stock
$1/2$ cup red wine vinegar
Salt to taste

CRANBERRY CHUTNEY
1 pound frozen cranberries
$1^1/2$ cups sugar
$1/2$ cup distilled white vinegar
1 cinnamon stick

CELERY ROOT PUREE
$1/2$ head celery root, washed and chopped
1 cup milk
1 cup cream
1 teaspoon caraway seeds
Salt to taste

APPLE FRISÉE SALAD
$1/2$ head frisée, yellow part only
2 slices Granny Smith apple, julienned
2 tablespoons extra virgin olive oil
1 teaspoon fresh lemon juice

PORK

1 Heat oil on high in a large, heavy Dutch oven.

2 Add pork belly and sear until browned on both sides.

3 Remove the pork.

4 Add the celery, onion, carrot, garlic, bay leaves, and peppercorns. Sweat for 6 minutes.

5 Put the pork back in the pot, add the wine and cook an additional 6 minutes.

6 Add the remaining ingredients, bring to a boil, and then reduce heat to low. Cover and cook until fork tender, about 1 to $1^1/_2$ hours.

7 When pork is done, strain the liquid through a cheesecloth and reduce by two-thirds, constantly skimming the grease that floats to the top.

CRANBERRY CHUTNEY

8 Place all ingredients in a saucepan and cook, stirring often, until liquid evaporates. Set aside in same saucepan.

CELERY ROOT PUREE

9 In a medium saucepan, place all ingredients and cook over medium heat until celery root is tender, about 20 minutes.

10 Drain, discard the liquid, and place all ingredients in a blender. Process to a smooth puree.

APPLE FRISÉE SALAD

11 Mix all ingredients in a bowl and set aside.

12 Portion the pork belly into 4 to 6 pieces.

TO SERVE

13 In a separate pot, place pork and reduced cooking liquid. Cook until hot and the broth is reduced to sauce consistency.

14 In a separate pot, reheat the celery root puree.

15 In the same pot it was cooked in, reheat the cranberry chutney.

16 Swirl the puree on individual plates and place a dollop of chutney on top.

17 Place a portion of pork belly on top.

18 Arrange apple frisée salad around each dish.

19 To finish, drizzle with the sauce.

bagna cauda

Barbetta, Italian, courtesy of Team De Cuisine

Bagna cauda is a fall and winter dish served in the northern region of Piemonte on holiday eves, which are by custom meatless. It is a gregarious and festive dish, traditionally eaten from a chafing dish. Gathering around a table, guests pass the vegetable platter. Holding a slice of bread in the left hand to catch the drippings, each guest spears a bite-size piece of vegetable with his/her fork and dips it in the bagna cauda. When the slice of bread becomes saturated, that delectable morsel is eaten.

SERVES 8

1 loaf crusty Italian bread
2 (4-ounce) cans anchovies, drained
3 cups olive oil
4 cloves garlic, cut into slivers
3 tablespoons butter

RAW VEGETABLES (RINSED AND DRIED)
1 cardoon, hunch-backed, as white as possible, cut into 4-inch pieces*
4 carrots, cut into quarters
4 Belgian endive, cut into quarters
4 sweet red bell peppers, cut into quarters
1 cauliflower, broken into "dip-size" pieces

1 Slice bread into 1-inch slices and place on a serving plate.

2 Chop anchovies.

3 In a large heavy skillet, heat olive oil over medium heat.

4 Add anchovies and garlic and cook, stirring constantly, until the anchovies and garlic have disintegrated to a puree consistency, about 10 minutes.

5 Stir in butter and cook an additional 15 to 20 seconds.

6 Transfer to a chafing dish and keep bagna cauda barely simmering, not boiling.

7 See headnote for serving.

* Artichoke hearts can be substituted.

zanzibar tuna tartare

Zanzibar, African, courtesy of Raul Bravo

Yellowfin is a red meaty tuna, ideal for tartare. Cut into tiny pieces, the meat is translucent. When serving fish raw, always purchase it from a reputable fishmonger to ensure high quality.

SERVES 4

TUNA TARTARE
6 ounces yellowfin tuna
1 tablespoon chili oil
Salt to taste

VINAIGRETTE
$1/2$ cup light soy sauce
$1 1/2$ teaspoons sugar
6 tablespoons lemon juice
3 tablespoons lime juice
$1/2$ teaspoon chili oil

AVOCADO SALAD
1 ripe avocado
1 tablespoon chopped red onion
1 tablespoon lime juice
$1/2$ teaspoon salt

GARNISH
Jalapeño pepper, sliced paper thin
Cilantro leaves

TUNA TARTARE

1 Dice the tuna into $1/4$-inch pieces and season with the chili oil and salt. Set aside.

VINAIGRETTE

2 In a mixing bowl, combine all ingredients and mix well until sugar is dissolved. For best results, the bowl and ingredients should be very cold.

AVOCADO SALAD

3 Peel and mash the avocado, leaving small chunks. Mix with the rest of the ingredients.

TO SERVE

4 On 4 small plates, divide avocado salad and top with the tuna mixture.

5 Drizzle the vinaigrette around the tuna and avocado.

6 Garnish with sliced jalapeño peppers and cilantro leaves.

7 Serve chilled.

deep-fried panko-crusted artichoke hearts with horseradish dip

Hudson Yards Cafe, Traditional American, courtesy of Jimmy Reardon

This easy-to-make treat is great for any type of gathering—large or small. Because of their coarse texture, Japanese panko absorb less oil than regular bread crumbs.

SERVES 4

4 cups vegetable oil
4 eggs
1/2 cup milk
Salt and pepper to taste
1–2 cups panko bread crumbs
3 (13.75-ounce) cans artichoke hearts

HORSERADISH DIP
1 cup whole mayonnaise
1/2 cup prepared white horseradish (more or less to taste)

1 Heat oil in a large, heavy pot to 365 degrees F.

2 In a bowl, whisk together the eggs, milk and salt and pepper.

3 Put panko in a separate bowl.

4 Dip artichoke hearts in the batter and roll in panko until thoroughly coated.

5 In batches, carefully place artichoke hearts in oil and fry, turning frequently, until golden brown.

6 Remove hearts and drain on paper towels.

7 Blend mayonnaise and horseradish and place in a 2-cup serving bowl.

8 Cut fried artichoke hearts in half and arrange on a serving platter.

9 Serve with the horseradish dip.

samosas with potato and peas

Bombay Eats, Indian, courtesy of Prakash Hundalani

This common snack in India can be traced back to Central Asia in the tenth century. While this recipe is vegetarian, these deep-fried samosas can be filled with a large variety of ingredients and served with chutney.

SERVES 4

$1/2$ pound white potatoes, peeled and diced
$3/4$ cup frozen green peas

2 tablespoons corn oil
1 medium onion, chopped
$1/2$ teaspoon chopped cumin seeds
$1/2$ teaspoon ground ginger
$1/2$ teaspoon turmeric
$1/2$ teaspoon garam masala
$1/2$ teaspoon salt
Juice from 1 lemon

1 cup all-purpose flour
2 teaspoons salt
2 tablespoons butter
2 tablespoons milk

Vegetable oil for deep frying
2 tablespoons chopped fresh cilantro for garnish

1 In a saucepan, boil potatoes until tender.

2 Drain well, return to saucepan and mash.

3 Cook peas in boiling water 3 to 4 minutes and drain well.

4 Heat the 2 tablespoons oil in a large heavy skillet over medium-high heat. Add onion, cumin, ginger, turmeric, garam masala and salt and cook 5 to 6 minutes, stirring occasionally.

5 Fold in potatoes, peas and lemon juice.

6 Remove from heat and allow to cool.

7 Sift flour and salt into a large bowl; cut in butter and blend until mixture resembles bread crumbs.

8 Add milk and knead to form a stiff dough. Divide dough into 6 pieces. Form each piece into a ball; roll on a floured surface to form a 6-inch circle. Cut each circle in half and divide filling among the pastries. With water, dampen the edge of each pastry, fold over to seal and form triangles to enclose filling.

9 In a heavy pot, heat 2 inches vegetable oil to 375 degrees F. In batches, fry samosas until golden brown, 4 to 5 minutes. Remove and drain on paper towels. Sprinkle with fresh cilantro.

curried crisped oysters with coconut wasabi dip

B. Smith, Global Eclectic, courtesy of B. Smith

The combination of coconut milk, curry powder and wasabi gives this delicious Southern fried oyster dish an exotic Eastern flavor. When purchasing the oysters, look for those packed in a clear liquid rather than milky.

SERVES 4

2 dozen oysters
1 1/2 cups all-purpose flour
1 1/2 teaspoons dried thyme leaves
1 1/2 teaspoons curry powder
1 teaspoon Old Bay Seasoning
3/4 teaspoon freshly ground black pepper
1/4 teaspoon cayenne pepper
Salt to taste
1 cup vegetable oil

COCONUT WASABI DIP
1/2 cup coconut milk
1/2 cup mayonnaise
2 teaspoons wasabi powder

1 Drain the oysters and pat dry with paper towels.

2 Stir together the flour, thyme, curry powder, Old Bay, black pepper, cayenne pepper and salt on a plate.

3 In a skillet over medium-high heat, heat the oil.

4 Dredge each oyster in the seasoned flour, shaking off excess. Set aside on a piece of waxed paper.

5 Cook the oysters in batches, 1 to 2 minutes on each side, until golden brown. Don't overcrowd the pan and don't overcook the oysters. Drain on a brown paper–covered rack.

COCONUT WASABI DIP

6 Whisk the ingredients together and refrigerate until ready to serve.

7 To plate, place a small ramekin of Coconut Wasabi Dip on each plate and place 6 oysters around the ramekin.

pebre salsa

Pomaire, Chilean, courtesy of Denic Catalan

Argentina has its chimichurri and Chile has its pebre. Traditionally served with bread for dipping, this Chilean staple is also a great accompaniment to meat, poultry and fish.

1 cup tomatoes, peeled, seeded and finely diced
1 cup finely chopped yellow onion
1/4 cup finely chopped fresh cilantro leaves
2 teaspoons corn oil
1 teaspoon finely chopped garlic
1 teaspoon red wine vinegar
1 red hot chile pepper, finely chopped
1/2 cup hot water
Salt and black pepper to taste

1 Blend all ingredients in a nonreactive bowl and refrigerate.

2 For maximum flavor, pebre should be served the same day it is made.

NINTH AVENUE INTERNATIONAL FOOD FESTIVAL

Hell's Kitchen is the home of an annual food celebration held in mid-May. It runs along Ninth Avenue between West 34th and West 57th streets and attracts millions from around the world to experience an amazing banquet. Not only do tourists join in the eating marathon, but they also receive a bonus: the interaction with the locals who are carrying on the tradition of their grandparents' and great-grandparents' work ethic and joy of sharing through food, drink and music.

grilled pepper shrimp with avocado, grapefruit and fennel salad

West Bank Cafe, Progressive American, courtesy of Joe Marcus

The combination of sweet, tart and peppery flavors make this light, refreshing appetizer ideal for spring and summer entertaining.

SERVES 4

16 large shrimp, deveined
Salt and pepper to taste
Olive oil for brushing shrimp

2 heads fennel
16 mint leaves, julienned
8 grapefruit segments
1 avocado, thinly sliced
1 tablespoon seeded and finely diced jalapeño
1 tablespoon fresh lime juice
1/2 cup olive oil
Salt and pepper to taste

1 Season the shrimp with salt and pepper, using more pepper than salt.

2 Brush shrimp with olive oil and, on a stovetop grill, grill shrimp about 2 minutes on each side, until opaque but not dry.

3 Shave the fennel head paper thin on a Japanese mandoline.

4 Toss together the fennel, mint, grapefruit, avocado, jalapeño, lime juice and olive oil.

5 Season with salt and pepper.

6 Divide salad among four plates and top with four shrimp each.

broccoli rapa e salsiccia

Cascina Ristorante, Italian, courtesy of Gualtiero Carosi

Also known as "rapini," broccoli rabe is a slightly bitter, mustard-flavored vegetable that is more closely related to turnips than broccoli. Once thought to be an ethnic Italian vegetable, it is now readily available and easily prepared. Always look for small stems and crisp leaves when shopping.

**SERVES 4 AS AN APPETIZER OR
2 AS AN ENTRÉE**

1 pound broccoli rabe, washed and drained
2 tablespoons olive oil
4 cloves garlic, smashed
Salt and freshly ground pepper to taste

2 large hot Italian sausages

1 Preheat oven to 350 degrees F.

2 In a large pot of boiling salted water, cook broccoli rabe for 1 minute. Drain well.

3 In a large heavy skillet, heat olive oil over medium-high heat and sauté broccoli rabe with garlic. Season with salt and pepper. Set aside.

4 Split the sausages lengthwise and pound them thin. Grill 1 to $1^{1}/_{2}$ minutes on each side.

5 Spread the broccoli rabe in a terra-cotta dish or round ovenproof casserole and spiral sausage on top.

6 Bake 5 to 10 minutes.

7 Serve in the casserole dish.

galette charleroi

Sortie, Belgian, courtesy of Akin Dawodu

This Belgian galette differs from the classic crêpe in the use of buckwheat rather than all-purpose flour. Buckwheat flour has a nutty and robust flavor that lends itself to savory dishes, especially cheese. Extra galettes can be wrapped in plastic and refrigerated 2 to 3 days or frozen for 1 month.

YIELDS ABOUT 12–14 GALETTES

GALETTES
1 cup whole milk
1 cup buckwheat flour
6 tablespoons water
2 whole eggs plus 2 yolks
$1/4$ teaspoon salt
1 tablespoon sugar
3 tablespoons butter, melted
Oil for pan

CHARLEROI FILLING
$3/4$ cup grated Parmesan cheese
$3/4$ cup grated Romano cheese
$1/2$ cup crushed walnuts

GALETTES

1 In a food processor or blender, place all ingredients and blend until smooth, about 10 seconds.

2 Pour into a covered container and refrigerate 1 to 2 hours.

3 Heat a 10-inch skillet over medium-high heat and lightly brush with vegetable oil or butter.

4 Pour $1/4$ cup batter onto skillet, tilting side to side to evenly distribute batter.

5 Cook 50 to 60 seconds, until first side is golden brown. Flip and cook 30 to 35 seconds, until second side is golden brown.

6 Transfer crêpe to a plate and continue with remaining crêpe batter.

7 Crêpes can be wrapped in plastic and refrigerated 2 to 3 days or frozen for 1 month.

CHARLEROI FILLING

8 Follow the procedure for the galette making. Once you flip the galette, evenly sprinkle it with 3 tablespoons Parmesan cheese, 3 tablespoons Romano cheese and 2 tablespoons crushed walnuts. Fold the galette into an "envelope," flip and cook about 50 to 60 seconds.

papa rellena con picadillo

Old San Juan, Puerto Rican/Argentinean, courtesy of Victor Rodriguez

The coating for these Puerto Rican stuffed potato balls calls for panko bread crumbs. These Japanese bread crumbs are the product of dried bread that is grated into fluffy, crispy flakes. They add more crunch because they absorb less oil than regular bread crumbs.

YIELDS 6 BALLS

POTATOES
2 pounds baking, or russet, potatoes, peeled, cut
   into 2-inch pieces
1 tablespoon salt
$1/2$ cup warm heavy cream
$1/4$ bunch fresh chives
4 tablespoons butter ($1/2$ stick)
Salt and white pepper to taste

PICADILLO
$1/2$ pound ground sirloin
$1/2$ small onion, chopped
$1/2$ small red pepper, chopped
$1/2$ small green pepper, chopped
$1/2$ small plum tomato, chopped
1 tablespoon chopped fresh cilantro
Salt and white pepper to taste

POTATO BALLS
1 cup all-purpose flour
2 eggs, slightly beaten
1–$1/2$ cups panko (Japanese bread crumbs)
Vegetable oil for deep frying

POTATOES

1 Put potatoes in a 5-quart pot. Add enough water to cover by 1 inch. Add 1 tablespoon salt. Bring to a simmer and cook, uncovered, until potatoes are tender, about 15 to 20 minutes.

2 When cooked, mash and add remaining five ingredients. Set aside and keep warm.

PICADILLO

3 In a large heavy skillet, brown meat. Drain and return to skillet.

4 Mix in the onion, peppers, tomato and cilantro and cook until vegetables are crisp-tender.

5 Season with salt and white pepper to taste.

POTATO BALLS

6 Divide mashed potatoes into 6 patties (about $1/2$ cup each).

7 Place a generous tablespoon of picadillo in the center of each patty. Gather potato around picadillo to enclose.

8 Coat each potato ball with flour. Dip in egg and then roll in panko.

9 In a deep fryer or a 5- to 6-quart heavy pot, heat oil to 365 degrees F.

10 In batches, fry croquettes (balls) until crisp and brown, about 5 to 6 minutes, turning occasionally.

11 Serve immediately.

hazelnut-crusted scotch eggs

Landmark Tavern, Irish, courtesy of Francisco Velazco

Scotch eggs have been popular pub fare in the British Isles for centuries. Hell's Kitchen's Landmark Tavern, dating from 1868, has given this treat a more complex flavor by adding ground hazelnuts to the bread crumbs. The nuts can be ground in a dry food processor work bowl, but care must be taken to avoid making paste through overprocessing.

SERVES 4

16 ounces ground Irish sausage
8 hard-boiled eggs, peeled
1/2 cup all-purpose flour
2 eggs, slightly beaten
1 1/2 cups bread crumbs
1/2 cup finely chopped hazelnuts
Vegetable oil for deep frying

1 Moisten hands with cold water to prevent sausage from sticking to your hands.

2 Divide sausage into 8 equal patties.

3 Place one egg on each patty and gather sausage around egg to enclose.

4 Coat each sausage-wrapped egg with flour, roll in beaten egg, and then roll in bread crumbs mixed with hazelnuts.

5 Heat 3 inches vegetable oil to 350 degrees F in a deep, heavy pot.

6 In batches, fry the eggs until the sausage is golden brown, about 5 to 6 minutes.

7 Serve on a bed of baby greens with an assortment of mustards.

8 Scotch eggs can be served hot, at room temperature or cold.

fresh goat cheese "ravioli" and ginger jus

Chez Josephine, French, courtesy of Richard Pimms

Rather than making pasta dough from scratch, store-bought wonton wrappers from Asian markets and some supermarkets make this delicious and impressive appetizer a snap to make.

SERVES 6

RAVIOLI
5 ounces fresh goat cheese (chèvre)
1/4 cup finely chopped fresh dill
Salt and freshly ground pepper to taste
1 package wonton wrappers

GINGER JUS
1 teaspoon canola oil
1 shallot, peeled and sliced
1 clove garlic, smashed
1/4 yellow onion, peeled and sliced
1 tablespoon coarsely chopped fresh ginger
1/2 teaspoon chili flakes
1/2 teaspoon fennel seeds
1/4 cup dry white wine
2 cups rich chicken stock
Salt and freshly ground pepper to taste
1 tablespoon butter

GARNISH
1/4 cup toasted pine nuts
2 teaspoons minced fresh chives

1 Combine cheese and dill and season with salt and pepper.

2 Lay 5 wonton wrappers at a time on a cool work surface. Place one teaspoon of chèvre mixture on the center of each wonton wrapper.

3 With the tip of your finger, slightly wet edges of wonton wrapper with cold water. Fold two corners of wrapper together and press to seal.

4 Bring remaining corners to meet the previous two and seal.

5 Repeat until there are 30 raviolis.

GINGER JUS

6 In a heavy saucepan over medium heat, heat canola oil. Add shallot, garlic, onion and ginger and cook until vegetables are translucent and tender.

7 Add the chili flakes, fennel seeds and white wine and cook until wine evaporates.

8 Cover with stock and bring to a boil. Lower heat and simmer until reduced by half.

9 Strain through a fine mesh strainer and set aside. Adjust for salt and pepper.

TO COMPLETE THE DISH

10 In a large pot, cook ravioli in boiling salted water for 2 minutes. Drain well.

11 In a small saucepan, heat Ginger Jus and whisk in butter.

12 Toss ravioli with ginger jus and place 5 wontons on individual plates.

13 Garnish with pine nuts and chives.

SOUPS & STEWS

My father opened our fish market in 1918, right after World War I. Back in the 1930s, I was one of the few Italian kids in a predominantly Irish neighborhood, but I had a lot of Irish friends. And I was happy because on St. Patrick's Day I ate as many free corned beef sandwiches as I could handle. My son and I still keep my father's market going, and I can't imagine doing anything else.

—Joe DeMartino
DeMartino's Fish Market

cucumber soup

Gazala Place, Druze, courtesy of Gazala Halabi

While soups are generally thought of as liquidy, this Druze soup has a thick, milky consistency characteristic of Druze cuisine in Israel, Jordan and Syria. Cool and mellow with mint and yogurt, this cold soup makes a refreshing summertime delight.

SERVES 4–6

2 large cucumbers, peeled
2 cloves garlic, minced
8 fresh mint leaves, finely chopped
2 cups plain yogurt
Salt to taste

1 Cut cucumbers in half lengthwise. With a spoon, scrape out the seeds and discard.

2 Cut the cucumbers in $1/2$-inch dice.

3 In a bowl, combine cucumbers with the remaining ingredients and blend well.

4 For a thinner consistency, gradually add more yogurt.

5 Serve chilled.

LANDMARK TAVERN

Built in 1868 by Patrick Henry Carley, this establishment was an Irish saloon on the first floor and home to the Carley family on the second and third floors. It is one of the oldest continually operating taverns in New York City. The pub closed for 30 minutes during Prohibition while they moved upstairs. Rumor has it that off-duty Irish cops rolled in the contraband beer barrels. Back then, lunch was free with the purchase of a five-cent beer. Prices have changed, but patrons still sit at the mahogany bar made from a single tree and munch on Hazelnut-Crusted Scotch Eggs (see page 38).

guinness beef stew

Landmark Tavern, Irish, courtesy of Francisco Velazco

Dark, dry Irish stout gives a rich, roasty flavor to this beef tenderloin stew. This version also combines red wine and veal stock, further intensifying the tastiness of this winter comfort food.

SERVES 6

MARINADE
2 cups Guinness beer
$1/2$ cup wine
$1/4$ cup olive oil
1 cup chopped parsley
2 cloves garlic
1 teaspoon salt
1 teaspoon freshly ground black pepper

BEEF STEW
1 ($2^{1}/_{2}$-pound) beef tenderloin, cut into 1-inch chunks
Salt and pepper to taste
3 tablespoons olive oil
4 shallots, chopped
1 cup red wine
1 cup Guinness beer
2 cups veal stock
3 tablespoons butter
3 tablespoons flour

MARINADE

1 Combine marinade ingredients well; add meat and marinate in the refrigerator 6 to 24 hours.

BEEF STEW

2 Drain beef and reserve liquid. Pat beef cubes dry with paper towels and season with salt and pepper.

3 In a heavy Dutch oven, heat olive oil over medium-high heat.

4 In batches, sear beef until browned on all sides, about 2 to 4 minutes.

5 Remove beef with a slotted spoon and set aside.

6 Add shallots to the pot and cook over medium heat until lightly browned.

7 Stir in red wine, beer, veal stock and the reserved marinade.

8 Return meat to the pot. There should be enough liquid to just cover the meat. If not, add more stock.

9 Bring to a boil, reduce heat and simmer, uncovered, 10 to 12 minutes.

10 In the meantime, using a fork, cream the butter and flour into a smooth paste. Add to the stew, blend well and bring to a boil. Reduce heat and simmer, uncovered, an additional 10 to 12 minutes. (Do not overcook, as tenderloin will fall apart.)

11 Season to taste with salt and pepper.

chez josephine french onion soup

Chez Josephine, French, courtesy of Richard Pimms

This classic French soup, known around the world, is the ultimate comfort food with its browned, crusty layer of broiled Gruyère and Parmesan cheeses. Onions cooked in a rich veal stock intensify the flavor.

SERVES 6

$^1/_2$ cup (1 stick) unsalted butter
5 yellow onions, peeled and sliced
5 leeks, white part only, split and sliced $^1/_4$ inch thick
10 shallots, peeled and sliced
2 bay leaves
5 sprigs fresh thyme
1 gallon veal stock*
Salt and pepper to taste
Toasted baguette croutons (recipe follows)
1 cup grated Gruyere cheese
$^1/_3$ cup freshly grated Parmesan cheese

BAGUETTE CROUTONS
1 baguette
Extra virgin olive oil
Garlic, minced
Salt and pepper

* Rich chicken stock can be substituted for veal stock.

1 In a large heavy stockpot, melt butter over low heat. Add onions, leeks and shallots and cook until caramelized. Add bay leaves and thyme.

2 Add veal stock, enough to cover onions.

3 Reduce heat and simmer to reduce by one-fourth.

4 Season with salt and pepper.

5 Place 2 croutons in individual broiler-proof soup crocks and ladle soup to fill.

6 Blend Gruyère and Parmesan thoroughly and generously cover soup.

7 Place under broiler to melt and brown cheese.

BAGUETTE CROUTONS

8 Slice a baguette into $^1/_2$-inch pieces. Brush with extra virgin olive oil, sprinkle with minced garlic, salt and pepper and bake in a 300-degree-F preheated oven until lightly toasted and dried.

coda alla vaccinara
Cascina Ristorante, Italian, courtesy of Gualtiero Carosi

This Roman oxtail stew received its name from Roman slaughterhouse workers, *vaccinari*, who were partially paid with the humble rejected oxtails. This poor man's meal was so luscious that it was elevated to a popular Italian dish.

SERVES 4–6

2 tablespoons extra virgin olive oil
1 carrot, finely chopped
1 large onion, finely chopped
1 celery stalk, finely chopped
2 cloves garlic, minced
2 bay leaves

4 pounds beef oxtail, cut into 12 pieces
Salt and freshly ground pepper to taste

1 cup dry white wine
1 tablespoon bitter cocoa powder
8 cups unsalted vegetable stock
1 pound tomatoes, peeled and chopped

1 teaspoon salt
1 carrot, cut into 1/4-inch julienne strips
1 celery stalk, cut into 1/4-inch julienne strips
2 tablespoons olive oil
Salt and pepper to taste

1 In a large, ovenproof Dutch oven, heat 2 tablespoons olive oil over medium heat. Add carrot, onion, celery, garlic and bay leaves and heat mixture until vegetables begin to sweat.

2 Sprinkle oxtails with salt and pepper and add the pieces to the pot.

3 Add wine and cook until the wine evaporates, about 10 to 15 minutes.

4 Stir in the cocoa powder and vegetable stock.

5 Preheat oven to 350 degrees F.

6 Cover the Dutch oven and bake for 2 hours. If there is too much liquid, heat uncovered on stovetop until excess stock evaporates.

7 Add tomatoes; cover and cook in oven an additional 40 minutes, stirring occasionally.

8 In a 2 1/2-quart saucepan, boil 4 cups water with 1 teaspoon salt.

9 Add carrot and celery sticks and boil until al dente, about 2 minutes. Drain.

10 In a heavy skillet, heat 2 tablespoons olive oil and sauté julienne vegetables until crisp-tender, about 2 to 3 minutes. Season with salt and pepper.

11 Remove oxtail pieces from pot and keep warm.

12 Put sauce in a blender and puree.

13 Place 2 to 3 oxtail pieces on individual plates. Cover generously with sauce. Garnish with julienne strips. Serve immediately.

pistou soup

Marseille, South of France, courtesy of Peter Larsen

Pistou is the French version of the Italian "pesto" and differs in that it does not include any nuts. It is traditional to pass the pistou and allow each guest to add according to his or her taste.

SERVES 4–6

SOUP

$1/3$ cup white beans (French coco or cranberry beans)
Salt to taste
2 tablespoons olive oil
1 cup onion cut in $1/2$-inch dice
$1/2$ cup carrot cut in $1/2$-inch dice
$1/2$ cup celery cut in $1/2$-inch dice
$1/2$ cup turnip cut in $1/2$-inch dice
$1/2$ cup chopped garlic
3 cups water
$1/2$ tablespoon salt
3 cups butternut squash in $1/2$-inch dice
1 cup zucchini in $1/2$-inch dice
1 cup peeled potato in $1/2$-inch dice
$3/4$ cup green beans in $1/2$-inch dice
1 sage leaf
1 bay leaf
1 cup fava beans (cooked and shelled)
12 Swiss chard leaves, chopped
$1/4$ cup grated Parmesan cheese for garnish

PISTOU

2 cloves garlic
2 cups packed basil
$1/4$ cup grated Parmesan cheese
$1/4$ cup grated Comté* cheese
2 cups olive oil (more or less, depending on desired thickness)
$1/2$ beefsteak tomato, peeled and seeded
Salt
* Gruyère can be substituted.

1 Soak beans in water overnight.

2 Drain beans and, over low heat, slowly simmer in 2 quarts unsalted water for 40 minutes. Season with salt. Beans should be halfway cooked. Set aside beans in their cooking liquid.

3 In an 8-quart heavy pot, heat olive oil over medium-low heat and cook onion, carrot, celery, turnip and garlic for 10 minutes. Do not brown.

4 Add 3 cups water and salt and simmer for 20 minutes.

5 Add squash, zucchini, potato, green beans, sage leaf, bay leaf and the reserved beans and cooking liquid.

6 Simmer, uncovered, until vegetables are tender and soup has thickened.

7 Add the fava beans and Swiss chard leaves.

8 Sprinkle Parmesan over soup.

PISTOU

9 Blend all ingredients in a food processor. Serve in a bowl for passing.

dublin lamb stew

P. D. O'Hurley's, Irish, courtesy of Paul Loftus

Moist, flavorful lamb is boiled and then simmered in stock with fresh vegetables for a great springtime dinner or a comfort food all year round.

SERVES 4–6

2 pounds lamb shoulder or leg, cut in 1-inch cubes
6–8 cups chicken stock
4 large white potatoes, cut into 1^{1}/$_{2}$-inch cubes
3 celery stalks, cut into 2-inch pieces
3 carrots, peeled and cut into 2-inch pieces
2 large onions, quartered
Salt and pepper to taste

1 Put lamb in a large Dutch oven and cover with water by 1 inch.

2 Bring to a boil, lower heat and simmer 15 to 20 minutes.

3 Strain lamb and wash with cold water.

4 Return to pot and add enough chicken stock to cover by 1 inch.

5 Bring to a boil, reduce heat and simmer an additional 15 to 20 minutes.

6 Add potatoes, celery, carrots, onions, salt and pepper and simmer until lamb is tender and vegetables are cooked, 15 to 20 minutes.

7 Season with salt and pepper.

NOTE: Add more stock during cooking process, if needed.

PICCININI BROTHERS

In the Roaring Twenties, half-brothers Guido Vaccari and Mauro Piccinini opened a retail butcher business in the heart of Hell's Kitchen to supply New York City's restaurants. The new store had one of the city's first walk-in freezers as well as a white enameled Toledo scale, which today sits proudly in the window. Grandsons Peter and Paul Vaccari can be found every day in the store, continuing the thriving family business and tradition.

kotosoupa avgolemono

Uncle Nick's Greek Cuisine, Greek, courtesy of Antonio Manatakis

Known as the "Greek penicillin," this brothy Mediterranean egg and lemon soup is refreshing, light and delicious and guaranteed to cure what ails you.

SERVES 6–8

SOUP
1 whole chicken, 3$^1/_2$ pounds
10 cups water
6 tablespoons olive oil
2 small carrots
1 small onion, quartered
Salt and pepper to taste
$^3/_4$ cup short grain rice

AVGOLEMONO
3 egg whites
$^1/_2$ cup fresh lemon juice

SOUP

1 Wash the chicken in and out under cold running water. Place in a large stockpot and add enough water to cover the chicken.

2 Slowly bring to a boil, skimming off scum from the top.

3 Add olive oil, carrots, onion, salt and pepper. Cover and simmer until chicken is tender and cooked through.

4 Remove chicken and vegetables and strain stock into another clean pot.

5 Bring strained stock to a boil, add rice and stir well.

6 Cover, reduce heat, and simmer 25 to 30 minutes, until rice is cooked.

AVGOLEMONO (EGG AND LEMON SAUCE)

7 Whisk egg whites until they form peaks. Gradually add lemon juice, beating continuously with a whisk.

8 Gradually pour 2 cups of the hot soup into the egg and lemon, constantly beating.

9 Pour the sauce into the soup, stirring constantly.

vegetarian mulligatawny soup

Bombay Eats, Indian, courtesy of Prakash Hundalani

Considered the national dish of India, this soup is "pepper water," *mulligu* meaning "pepper" and *thanni* meaning "water," although pepper plays a very small part in the dish. Mulligatawny is traditionally vegetarian, but British colonialists often added chicken.

SERVES 4

2 tablespoons butter
1 large onion, finely chopped

1 tablespoon coriander
1 whole dried chili
1 teaspoon turmeric
$1/4$ teaspoon cayenne
$1/4$ teaspoon kosher salt

4 cups vegetable stock
2–3 plum tomatoes, chopped
1 large potato, unpeeled and cut in 1-inch cubes
1 large green bell pepper, finely chopped
1 stalk celery, cut into $1/2$-inch slices
1 large carrot, peeled and finely sliced
1 (14-ounce) can coconut milk

2 tablespoons fresh lemon juice
1 tablespoon minced fresh parsley
1 tablespoon minced fresh cilantro
Salt and pepper to taste

1 In a large Dutch oven, heat butter over medium heat. Add onion and cook until transparent but not browned.

2 Stir in the coriander, chili, turmeric, cayenne and salt and cook 2 to 3 minutes, until well incorporated.

3 Stir in stock and vegetables, lower heat and simmer 10 to 15 minutes.

4 Blend in coconut milk and cook an additional 5 minutes. Remove from heat and cool several minutes.

5 Remove the whole chili and discard.

6 Blend the soup with a hand blender or, in batches, in a jar blender. Do not overblend, as there should be a slight texture.

7 Stir in the lemon juice, parsley and cilantro and allow to sit for 45 minutes to allow the flavors to intensify. Add salt and pepper to taste.

8 Reheat over low heat and serve.

tom kha gai

Olieng, Thai, courtesy of Nid Euashachai

Thai ingredients come together in this multiflavored soup. Once considered exotic and hard to find, lemongrass, kaffir lime leaves and galangal are now readily available in some supermarkets and in all Asian markets.

SERVES 2–4

1 cup chicken broth
1 cup unsweetened coconut milk
4 pieces lemongrass
6 pieces kaffir lime leaves
4 pieces galangal
$1/2$ cup straw mushrooms
$1/2$ cup white mushrooms, sliced
1 cup thinly sliced uncooked chicken breast
4 tablespoons fish sauce
1 teaspoon sugar
6 tablespoons fresh lime juice
2 tablespoons chopped cilantro

1 In a large, heavy pot, combine chicken broth, coconut milk, lemongrass, kaffir lime leaves and galangal. Bring to a boil.

2 Add mushrooms, chicken, fish sauce, sugar and lime juice.

3 Simmer for 5 minutes.

4 Ladle into soup bowls and sprinkle with cilantro.

aztecan black bean soup

El Azteca, Mexican, courtesy of Maria Dias

Mexican favorites merge to give intense flavor to this hearty comfort soup. Hot buttered cornbread is the perfect complement.

SERVES 4–6

1 pound black beans, washed and picked over

1 tablespoon corn oil
1 medium tomato, chopped
$1/4$ cup chopped yellow onion
$1/4$ cup green bell pepper
$1/2$ teaspoon minced garlic
Salt and pepper to taste

GARNISH
Chopped cilantro
Sour cream

1 In a large heavy pot, add black beans and cover with water by 1 inch. Boil until tender, 45 minutes to 1 hour, adding water as needed to cover the beans. Stir occasionally to prevent sticking.

2 In a heavy skillet, heat corn oil over medium-high heat.

3 Add the tomato, onion, bell pepper, garlic and salt and pepper and cook 3 to 4 minutes.

4 When beans are tender, stir in the sautéed vegetables, reduce heat and simmer 4 to 5 minutes.

5 Adjust salt and pepper to taste.

GARNISH

6 Garnish with fresh cilantro and a dollop of sour cream.

farouk's crushed lentil soup

La Kabbr, Middle Eastern, courtesy of Farouk Mansoor

This hearty and healthy soup combines lentils and split peas with a delicious blend of Middle Eastern spices.

SERVES 6–8

2 tablespoons olive oil
1 medium onion, chopped
1 stalk celery, chopped
1 1/2 cups red lentils
1/2 cup dried green split peas
2 teaspoons salt
1/2 teaspoon black pepper
1/2 teaspoon cumin
1/2 teaspoon curry powder
8 cups chicken stock
1 cup broken vermicelli

1 In a large Dutch oven, heat olive oil over high heat. Add onion and celery and sauté 2 to 3 minutes.

2 Lower heat to medium and add the lentils, split peas, salt, pepper, cumin and curry powder. Cook 3 to 4 minutes, stirring constantly.

3 Add the chicken stock and simmer 30 to 40 minutes, or until lentils and peas are tender, stirring occasionally.

4 If necessary, add more stock to maintain soup consistency.

5 Add vermicelli and cook an additional 10 to 15 minutes.

6 Adjust seasoning to taste.

asapao andalucía

Cafe Andalucia, Spanish Tapas, courtesy of Guillermo Vidal

From the Andalucía region of Spain, this mussel and shrimp soup with rice is substantial enough to serve as a main course. A green salad and a loaf of crusty bread complete the meal.

SERVES 4

3 tablespoons olive oil
1 cup chopped yellow onion
1 cup chopped celery
3 plum tomatoes, coarsely chopped
6 cloves garlic, minced
16 mussels
6 cups vegetable stock
2 envelopes Goya "con Azafran" seasoning
2 cups cooked rice
16 shrimp (21–25 count), peeled and deveined

GARNISH
1/2 cup chopped cilantro

1 Heat oil in a 4-quart heavy pot.

2 Add onion, celery, tomatoes and garlic and sauté 2 to 3 minutes, until vegetables soften.

3 Add mussels, cover the pot and cook on high heat, shaking the pot occasionally, until mussels open, 6 to 8 minutes. Discard any unopened mussels.

4 Add stock and Goya seasoning and bring to a boil.

5 Add rice and continue to boil 1 to 2 minutes.

6 Add shrimp and boil 1$1/2$ to 2 minutes.

GARNISH
7 Garnish with fresh cilantro.

russian borscht

Uncle Vanya Cafe, Russian, courtesy of Marina Troshina

Every country has its signature soup, and Russia's beet-based soup is known around the world. Served hot or cold and topped with a dollop of sour cream, borscht is a soul-satisfying meal.

SERVES 4–6

3 tablespoons vegetable oil
1 large onion, peeled and chopped
1 carrot, peeled and finely chopped
3 cloves garlic, chopped

2 medium beets, peeled and grated
2 medium russet, or baking, potatoes, peeled and cut into 1-inch chunks
2 tomatoes, peeled and chopped

3 cups shredded green cabbage
Beef stock or vegetable stock to cover by 1 inch
2 bay leaves
1 tablespoon red wine vinegar
1 teaspoon sugar
Salt and pepper to taste

GARNISH
Fresh chopped dill
Sour cream

1 In a large Dutch oven, heat vegetable oil over medium-high heat. Add onion, carrot and garlic and sauté 4 to 5 minutes.

2 Add beets, potatoes and tomatoes and cook over medium heat 8 to 10 minutes, stirring constantly, adding a little water if necessary to prevent sticking.

3 Add cabbage, stock, bay leaves, vinegar, sugar, salt and pepper.

4 Cook over medium-low heat and simmer 30 to 35 minutes.

5 Adjust seasoning.

GARNISH

6 Borscht can be served hot or cold.

7 Sprinkle with fresh dill and add a dollop of sour cream.

caldo verde

Rice 'n' Beans, Brazilian, courtesy of Maria Lemos

Linguiça is the Portuguese sausage that intensifies the flavor of this simple yet delicious Brazilian green soup. Thickened with mashed potatoes, the soup is poured over uncooked collard greens.

SERVES 4

2 pounds potatoes, peeled and cut in large chunks
5 1/2 cups chicken stock (divided)
1/2 pound linguiça sausage, sliced
1 tablespoon garlic
Salt and pepper to taste
6 leaves of collard greens, shredded
Olive oil

1 In a large pot of boiling, salted water, cook potatoes until tender, about 15 to 20 minutes. Drain and mash with 1/2 cup chicken stock. Set aside.

2 Use same pot to sauté sausage and garlic until lightly browned.

3 Add remaining 5 cups of stock and mashed potatoes. Season with salt and pepper.

4 In individual soup bowls, divide collard greens. Pour soup over the greens and drizzle lightly with olive oil. Add salt and pepper to taste.

molokhia

36 West, American/Egyptian, courtesy of Gabriel Neama

Molokhia, the national dish of Egypt, is a thick, sticky but utterly delicious and nutritious soup/stew. Its texture is due to the green, leafy plant molokhia, also known as Jew's Mallow because some believe it was prepared by ancient Jews. Frozen molokhia can be purchased in Middle Eastern or Asian grocery stores.

SERVES 6–8

1/2 cup salted butter
1/4 cup olive oil
6–8 cloves garlic, minced
3 quarts chicken stock
1/2 teaspoon ground coriander
2 (14-ounce) packages frozen molokhia
Salt and cayenne pepper to taste

2–3 cups cooked white rice

1 In a large stockpot, heat butter and olive oil over medium-high heat.

2 Add garlic and cook, stirring constantly, 1 to 2 minutes, until softened but not brown.

3 Stir in the chicken stock and bring to a boil.

4 Add the coriander and molokhia and again bring to a boil. Reduce heat and simmer 8 to 10 minutes. Season to taste with salt and pepper.

5 Serve over rice.

kartoffelsuppe

Hallo Berlin, German, courtesy of Rolf Babiel

France has its cold potato and leek soup (vichyssoise) and Germany has its hot version. Seasoned with marjoram and nutmeg, enriched with cream and dolloped with sour cream, kartoffelsuppe is a celebration of "peasant" ingredients.

SERVES 4–6

$^1/_4$ cup butter
1 leek, washed and cut into $^1/_2$-inch slices

6 cups chicken stock
4 large red potatoes, peeled and cut in 1-inch dice
1 teaspoon marjoram
$^1/_2$ teaspoon nutmeg
$^1/_2$ teaspoon granulated garlic
Salt and pepper to taste

1 cup half-and-half
2 tablespoons chopped fresh dill
Sour cream (optional)

1 In a large Dutch oven, melt butter over medium heat.

2 Add leek, cover and cook until tender, 10 to 15 minutes.

3 Stir in stock, potatoes, marjoram, nutmeg, garlic and salt and pepper.

4 Reduce heat to medium-low and simmer until potatoes are tender, 20 to 25 minutes.

5 Mash the potatoes in the pot to thicken the soup.

6 Stir in the half-and-half and fresh dill and simmer 4 to 5 minutes. Adjust seasoning.

7 Serve in individual soup bowls and top with a dollop of sour cream, if desired.

ajiaco

Pomaire, Chilean, courtesy of Denic Catalan

This hearty Chilean seasoned meat and potato soup is the perfect winter comfort meal. Garnished with hard-boiled eggs, ajiaco combines flavorful ingredients in a one-pot dish.

SERVES 6–8

1 (2-pound) eye of lean beef round
3 tablespoons olive oil

2 medium onions, sliced
2 cloves garlic, minced
1 tablespoon Spanish paprika
1 tablespoon dried thyme
1 tablespoon dried oregano
Salt and pepper to taste

8 cups beef stock
1 whole aji chile
1 pound potatoes, peeled

GARNISH
3 tablespoons fresh parsley, chopped
2 large hard-boiled eggs, finely chopped

1 Preheat oven to 375 degrees F.

2 Thoroughly rub the beef with olive oil and bake in a roasting pan for 30 minutes.

3 Cut meat into strips, return to pan and set aside.

4 Sauté onion, garlic, paprika, thyme, oregano, salt and pepper until onion is tender.

5 Add beef stock and bring to a boil.

6 Add chile, meat and juices. Simmer for 30 minutes.

7 Cut potatoes into lengthwise wedges. Add to soup and simmer for 15 minutes. Let rest off the heat for 10 minutes.

GARNISH

8 Serve in soup bowls and garnish with parsley and eggs.

minestrone di verdure

Mangia e Bevi, Italian, courtesy of Emmanuel Zitto

In this quintessential soup of Italy, spinach and peas replace the traditional beans and pasta, giving it a green color and a lighter, refreshing spring flavor.

SERVES 4

2 tablespoons olive oil
1 cup diced onion
1 cup coarsely chopped celery
$1/2$ cup peeled and coarsely chopped carrot
6 cups chicken stock
$1^1/2$ cups potatoes, peeled and cut into 1-inch dice
1 cup coarsely chopped fresh spinach
1 cup frozen green peas
Salt and pepper

1　Heat olive oil in a Dutch oven. Add onion, celery, and carrot and cook over medium-high heat until slightly softened.

2　Add stock and bring to a boil.

3　Lower heat, add potatoes, and simmer until tender, about 15 minutes.

4　Add spinach and peas and cook for 5 to 7 minutes.

5　Season to taste with salt and pepper.

lamb tagine with prunes, almonds and sesame seeds

Tagine Dining Gallery, Moroccan, courtesy of Hamid Idrissi

The term *tagine* refers to both the Moroccan stew and the North African conical-shaped casserole it's cooked in. This recipe uses a large heavy pot, as tagines are not common household equipment. The result is the same: moist lamb simmered in a sweet and pungent sauce and topped with the crunchiness of almonds and sesame seeds.

SERVES 4

3 tablespoons olive oil, divided
1$^1/_2$ pounds lamb, cut into 1$^1/_2$-inch cubes

1 large onion, sliced
1 large tomato, sliced
1 bunch cilantro, coarsely chopped

1 teaspoon sugar (optional)
1 teaspoon ground ginger
$^1/_2$ teaspoon white pepper
$^1/_2$ teaspoon paprika
$^1/_2$ teaspoon turmeric
$^1/_2$ teaspoon ground coriander seeds
$^1/_4$ teaspoon cinnamon
1 cup water

$^1/_2$ pound prunes
Sea salt to taste

3-4 cups cooked couscous

GARNISH
$^1/_4$ cup slivered almonds, toasted, for garnish
1 tablespoon sesame seeds, toasted, for garnish

1 In a 4–6-quart heavy pot, heat 2 tablespoons olive oil over medium-high heat. Brown lamb on all sides in batches, about 4 to 6 minutes for each batch. Set aside.

2 Heat remaining tablespoon olive oil in pot. Add onion and sauté until softened.

3 Return lamb to pot and add tomato and cilantro.

4 Dissolve sugar and spices in 1 cup water. Pour water with dissolved spices over the contents of the pot.

5 Stir and cook over low heat until boiling, about 10 to 15 minutes. Stir gently with a wooden spoon. Cover tightly and continue to cook 1 to 1$^1/_2$ hours. Add liquid during cooking if needed. Five minutes before serving, add the prunes.

6 Adjust seasoning and serve with couscous.

GARNISH

7 Sprinkle with toasted almonds and toasted sesame seeds.

feijoada

Rice 'n' Beans, Brazilian, courtesy of Maria Lemos

Considered the national dish of Brazil, feijoada is believed to have been introduced to Brazil by black slaves in the sixteenth century. Because of the heartiness of the stew, it is customary to eat it at lunch and indulge in a nap afterward. Feijoada is served with white rice, collard greens and orange slices, which are said to counter-act the fat of the pork.

SERVES 8–10

FEIJOADA

2 pounds black beans
$1/4$ cup olive oil
1 large yellow onion, chopped
6 cloves garlic, minced
3 bay leaves

1 pound pork belly
1 pound beef chuck, cut into $1/2$-inch cubes
1 pound linguiça (Portuguese sausage)
1 pound ham hocks
1 pound pork ribs, divided into 2-rib pieces
1 pound total: pig foot, ear, tail (optional)
$1/2$ pound carne seca (salt-cured beef)
$1/2$ pound slab bacon, rind removed and
   discarded

Hot sauce to taste
Orange slices for garnish

COLLARD GREENS

$1/4$ cup olive oil
5 cloves garlic, slivered
2 pounds collard greens, washed, dried and
   chopped into 2-inch pieces
Juice of one lemon
$1/4$–$1/2$ cup vegetable stock
Salt to taste, optional

3–4 cups cooked rice

FEIJOADA

1 Soak beans in a bowl of cold water over-night.

2 In a large, heavy skillet, heat olive oil over high heat. Add onion, garlic and bay leaves and sauté 3 to 4 minutes, stirring constantly.

3 Add beans and meats to the pot.

4 Add water to cover by 1 to 2 inches and bring to a boil.

5 Reduce heat to medium-low and simmer, uncovered, until beans are tender and meats are cooked, $1^1/2$ to 2 hours.

6 During cooking, stir occasionally, skimming off any foam that rises to the top, and add water as needed to cover the beans and meat.

7 Add hot sauce to taste. Serve orange slices on the side.

NOTE: Salt should be added only at the end and might not be necessary due to the saltiness of the meat.

COLLARD GREENS

8 In a large, heavy skillet, heat olive oil over medium-high heat.

9 Add garlic and sauté 2 to 3 minutes, stirring constantly to avoid burning.

10 Add collard greens, toss well with oil and garlic and sauté 2 to 3 minutes.

11 Combine lemon juice with stock. Lower heat to medium and gradually stir in stock.

12 Cook until greens are wilted and tender, 8 to 10 minutes.

SALADS

A few years ago when I was closing for the night and pulling down the gates at Landmark Tavern, I saw the curtains move. Thought it strange and checked the windows. They were shut tight. Then, I saw a little girl about ten with blonde hair in a white dress rocking back and forth on the threshold. The story had always been that a child died of cholera upstairs in the 1800s and her ghost remained. Never a believer, I made a quick exit saying, "The kitchen's closed, but help yourself!" As I hurried down the street, I had to smile, thinking, "It's true: once you live in Hell's Kitchen, you never want to leave."

—Denny Bess
Landmark Tavern

ethiopian tomato salad

Queen of Sheba, Ethiopian, courtesy of Philipos Mengistu

"Simple is best" is proven true in this African salad. The jalapeño sparks the subtle flavor of the tomato and onion and keeps in character with the spicy cuisine of Ethiopia.

SERVES 4

QUEEN OF SHEBA DRESSING
1/4 cup red wine vinegar
1/2 teaspoon salt to taste
1/4 teaspoon black pepper
1/2 cup olive oil

SALAD
1 1/2 pounds tomatoes, chopped in
  1/2-inch dice
1/2 red onion, finely chopped
1 jalapeño pepper, seeded and minced

1 Gently blend tomatoes, onion and jalapeño.

2 In a blender or with a wire whisk, briefly mix vinegar, salt and pepper. Gradually add oil in a steady stream until dressing emulsifies.

3 Adjust salt and pepper and fold dressing into the salad.

slow-roasted beet & arugula salad with sunflower vinaigrette

B. Smith, Global Eclectic, courtesy of B. Smith

The earthiness of the slow-roasted beets is enhanced by a simple-to-make balsamic reduction. While true balsamic vinegar is aged for twelve years and is expensive, there are many more-affordable brands available in supermarkets.

SERVES 4

4–5 medium-size fresh beets
3 tablespoons extra virgin olive oil
1 tablespoon plus 1 teaspoon red wine vinegar
1/4 cup unsalted toasted sunflower seeds
4 cups arugula, stems removed, rinsed and patted dry
1/4 cup walnut halves
1/4 cup crumbled soft goat cheese (chèvre or feta)
Salt and black pepper to taste
1 1/2 cups balsamic vinegar, for reduction (optional)

1　Preheat oven to 350 degrees F.

2　Wash the beets well and trim the roots and stems to 1 inch without piercing the skin.

3　Place the beets on a sheet of aluminum foil, fold into an airtight packet and place on a cookie sheet. Bake until tender, about 45 to 60 minutes.

4　Cool beets, remove skins, and cut into cubes. Cover and chill until ready to prepare salad.

5　Whisk together the olive oil, vinegar and sunflower seeds in a mixing bowl.

6　Toss arugula with the vinaigrette and divide among four salad plates.

7　Add beets and walnuts, and then crumble the goat cheese evenly over the top of each salad.

8　Season with salt and pepper.

OPTIONAL BALSAMIC REDUCTION

9　In a saucepan, heat vinegar over medium until slightly thickened and reduced to 2/3 cup. Drizzle the rim of each salad plate with reduction.

gurkensalat

Hallo Berlin, German, courtesy of Rolf Babiel

Favorite German ingredients of vinegar, dill and lemon combine in this refreshing and cooling cucumber salad. The dressing preparation is quick and is excellent with green beans as well as cucumbers.

DRESSING
2 tablespoons vegetable oil
1 tablespoon white vinegar
Juice from 1 lemon
2 tablespoons chopped fresh dill
$1/4$ cup chopped red bell pepper
$1/4$ cup chopped onion
$1/8$ teaspoon sugar
Salt and pepper to taste

5 medium cucumbers, peeled and thinly sliced

1 Mix dressing ingredients well. Pour over cucumbers and toss until well coated.

2 Refrigerate 30 to 40 minutes to allow flavors to blend.

grune bohnen salat

2 (16-ounce) packages frozen green beans
Dressing (recipe above)

1 Cook green beans according to package directions.

2 Chill well and toss with dressing.

meza luna salad

Hudson Yards Cafe, Traditional American, courtesy of Jimmy Reardon

This easy salad is made spectacular with its combination of vegetables, nuts, cheese and fruit. Grilled chicken slices can be added to create a light summertime main course.

SERVES 4

RASPBERRY VINAIGRETTE
1 cup raspberry vinegar
1/4 cup extra virgin olive oil
1/4 cup sugar
4 cloves garlic, crushed and minced
Salt and pepper

SALAD
8 cups mixed organic baby greens, washed and dried
1 medium red bell pepper, julienned
1 cup organic walnuts
1 cup imported bleu cheese
1/2 cup dried cranberries

RASPBERRY VINAIGRETTE

1 Whisk vinaigrette ingredients until thoroughly combined.

SALAD

2 In a large salad bowl, toss baby greens with the vinaigrette.

3 Gently fold in the sweet pepper, walnuts, bleu cheese and cranberries.

PADDY'S MARKET

After the Civil War, the food business became the essential support for the residents of Hell's Kitchen. Ninth Avenue, the main street in the neighborhood, was home to Paddy's Market. Begun in the 1880s, Paddy's was an immigrant pushcart market. The Irish, Italian and Greek merchants came from all over the neighborhood to sell their vegetables, meats, fruits, poultry, oils and spices, making the area a primary food source for the city of New York. In 1938, Paddy's was evicted to make way for the building of the Lincoln Tunnel. The vendors moved to two side streets off the avenue and remained during and after World War II. Sadly, by the 1950s, Paddy's Market had disappeared completely.

iraqi salad

La Kabbr, Middle Eastern, courtesy of Farouk Mansoor

Chopped salads are most popular throughout the Middle East, and the assortment of ingredients is limitless. Let your imagination take over, just remembering that all ingredients should be cut in easy-to-eat bites.

SERVES 4

VINAIGRETTE

5 tablespoons olive oil
1 tablespoon vegetable oil
$1/4$ cup red wine vinegar
Juice from 1 lemon

SALAD

1 cup cooked chickpeas
$1/4$ pound Romaine lettuce, cut in $1/2$-inch dice
1 small cucumber, peeled and cut in $1/2$-inch dice
1 large tomato, seeded and cut in $1/2$-inch dice
$1/2$ cup canned beets, cut in $1/2$-inch dice
Salt and freshly ground black pepper

VINAIGRETTE

1 Whisk all ingredients together until well blended.

SALAD

2 If using dried chickpeas, cook according to package directions. For canned chickpeas, drain, rinse and dry.

3 Gently toss all salad ingredients together.

4 Toss the salad with the vinaigrette and season with salt and freshly ground pepper.

shaved green papaya salad

Zanzibar, African, courtesy of Raul Bravo

The Thai chili, also known as the "bird pepper," heats up the sweet, creamy papaya in this multiflavored African salad. The fruity and sour characteristics of the tamarind add to the many taste sensations.

SERVES 4–6

DRESSING
2 teaspoons chopped garlic
6 teaspoons olive oil
1/2 teaspoon salt
1 Thai chili or other small red chili, diced
2 tablespoons sugar
1 tablespoon tamarind paste (can use tamarind concentrate)
2 teaspoons lime juice
1 teaspoon fish sauce

SALAD
2 ounces roasted raw cashews (no salt)
2 teaspoons olive oil
2 ounces long beans or haricots verts
Salt to taste
1 green papaya (approximately 1–2 pounds)
1/2 bunch cilantro leaves

DRESSING

1 Preheat oven to 350 degrees F.

2 In a sauté pan, sauté the garlic in the oil until soft. Put the garlic in a blender with the remaining ingredients and blend until smooth.

SALAD

3 Place the cashews on a baking sheet and roast for approximately 10 minutes in a preheated 350-degree-F oven. When cool, chop the cashews into small pieces.

4 In a sauté pan, heat the oil and sauté the long beans until soft. Season with salt and set aside to cool.

5 Peel the papaya with a potato peeler and shave the flesh into small strips. Set aside.

6 Remove the cilantro leaves from the stems and set aside.

7 To serve, combine all the ingredients (cashews, long beans, papaya and cilantro) in a bowl and toss with the dressing. Season with salt before serving.

NOTE: Thai chili peppers, fish sauce, long beans and tamarind paste are available in the Asian section of supermarkets or in any Asian market.

piyaz

Troy Turkish Grill, Turkish, courtesy of Nurettin Kirbiyic

This Turkish white bean salad is delicious and chock full of protein. Not only easy to prepare, it's a great make-ahead dish.

SERVES 4–6

2¹/₂–3 cups cooked white beans (great northern or cannellini)
1 large red onion, thinly sliced
4–5 tablespoons red wine vinegar
1¹/₂ cups flat-leaf parsley, finely chopped
Salt and pepper to taste

GARNISH
Hard-boiled eggs cut in wedges
Kalamata olives

1 If using dried beans, cook according to package directions. If using canned beans, drain, rinse and dry well.

2 Toss all ingredients, except eggs and olives, until well blended.

3 Serve at room temperature as a salad or side dish.

4 Garnish with eggs and olives.

insalata bianca

Mangia e Bevi, Italian, courtesy of Emmanuel Zitto

An Italian "white salad" with a light citrus dressing is a cinch to make but is high on flavor. This refreshing spring or summer salad easily becomes a main course with the addition of chicken or shrimp.

SERVES 4–6

3 small fennel bulbs
2–3 stalks celery
8 ounces white button mushrooms

$1/3$ cup extra virgin olive oil
2 tablespoons lemon juice
2 teaspoons lemon zest
$1/2$ teaspoon sugar
$1/4$ teaspoon salt
$1/8$ teaspoon pepper
$1/2$ cup Parmigiano-Reggiano cheese, or to taste

1 Thinly slice fennel, celery and mushrooms. (Using a Japanese mandoline is recommended.)

2 Combine olive oil, lemon juice, zest, sugar, salt and pepper in a blender or the work bowl of a food processor and blend until well combined.

3 Pour vinaigrette on salad ingredients and toss. Sprinkle cheese on salad just before serving.

salad "olivier"

Uncle Vanya Cafe, Russian, courtesy of Marina Troshina

French chef M. Olivier opened The Hermitage, a restaurant in Moscow, in the 1860s and created this classic Russian salad. While called a salad, it is substantial enough to be a complete meal. If the chicken is omitted, "Olivier" becomes a vegetarian dish.

SERVES 4–6

2 (6–8 ounce) boneless, skinless chicken breasts
1 whole onion, peeled and halved
2 teaspoons salt

1 pound red potatoes
2 medium cucumbers
1 cup frozen peas, thawed
2 hard-boiled eggs, coarsely chopped
1 medium onion
1 cup mayonnaise

GARNISH
8 sprigs parsley

1 Place chicken, onion and salt in a large pot and cover with water by 2 inches.

2 Bring to a simmer and cook until chicken is cooked, 8 to 12 minutes. Remove chicken and cool.

3 Boil potatoes in their skins until tender, 25 to 30 minutes. Remove and cool. When cooled, remove the skins.

4 Peel the cucumbers and cut into $1/2$-inch cubes.

5 Cut cooled chicken and potatoes into $1/2$-inch cubes.

6 In a large bowl, combine chicken, potatoes, cucumbers, peas, eggs and onion. Carefully fold in mayonnaise and blend but do not mash.

7 Refrigerate the salad until ready to serve, but not longer than 3 hours.

8 Garnish with parsley just before serving.

mixed green salad with bamboo ginger dressing

Bamboo 52, Japanese, courtesy of Kevin Wunkei Chan

Mixed greens reach a high level of flavor when tossed with a delectable multiflavored dressing combining fresh fruits and vegetables.

SERVES 4

BAMBOO GINGER DRESSING
3 celery sticks, chopped
2 tablespoons fresh ginger, chopped
1 carrot, diced
1/2 apple, peeled and diced
1/2 orange, peeled, seeded and chopped
1/2 lemon, peeled, seeded and chopped
1/2 onion, peeled and chopped
1/4 fresh pineapple, peeled and diced
1/2 cup vegetable oil
1/2 cup white vinegar
1 tablespoon sugar
1 teaspoon salt

SALAD
1/2 pound mixed greens
20 cherry tomatoes, halved, for garnish
Freshly ground black pepper, optional

BAMBOO GINGER DRESSING

1 **Place all ingredients in a blender and pulse until completely blended.**

2 **Add more sugar and salt to taste.**

SALAD

3 **Plate mixed greens and dress with vegetable/fruit dressing.**

4 **Top with cherry tomato halves and sprinkle with freshly ground pepper, if desired.**

tabbouleh

Troy Turkish Grill, Turkish, courtesy of Nurettin Kirbiyic

In the Middle East, salads, appetizers (meze) and side dishes are often interchangeable and offer great versatility. Regardless of the category, bulgur is flavored with the freshness of parsley, mint and lemon in this Turkish version.

SERVES 4

1 cup bulgur
2 large tomatoes, seeded and finely chopped
2 cups fresh parsley, finely chopped
1 cup fresh mint, finely chopped
$1/2$ cup olive oil
$1/2$ cup scallions, chopped
$1/4$ cup fresh lemon juice
Salt and pepper to taste

1 In a bowl, soak bulgur in $2^1/2$ cups boiling water. Cover and set aside for 20 to 30 minutes, until all liquid is absorbed. With paper towels, squeeze out excess water.

2 Place bulgur in a serving bowl and fold in remaining ingredients. Blend well and season to taste with salt and pepper.

3 Serve at room temperature.

becco's classic caesar salad

Becco, Italian, courtesy of Bill Gallagher

Created in 1924 by restaurateur Caesar Cardini, Caesar salad traditionally used a raw egg. In response to today's health concerns, this version of the famous salad uses a cooked egg yolk. The yolk disperses and the traditional taste sensation remains.

SERVES 6

CROUTONS
2 cups cubed ($1/2$ inch) firm-textured white bread

CAESAR DRESSING
2 tablespoons red wine vinegar, plus more for dressing the salad
2 tablespoons fresh lemon juice
4 cloves garlic
4 anchovy fillets
$1/3$ cup extra-virgin olive oil, or as needed
1 tablespoon Dijon mustard
1 hard-boiled egg yolk
$1/2$ teaspoon salt
Freshly ground black pepper
$1/4$ teaspoon Tabasco sauce
$1/2$ teaspoon Worcestershire sauce

SALAD
1 (18-ounce) package hearts of romaine, cut into 1-inch pieces
1 cup freshly grated Parmigiano-Reggiano cheese
Additional ungrated Parmigiano-Reggiano for shaving

CROUTONS

1 Preheat oven to 350 degrees F.

2 Spread bread cubes on a baking sheet and bake about 12 minutes, tossing once or twice, until cubes are golden brown. Remove and cool.

NOTE: Croutons can be prepared up to a day in advance and kept in an airtight container.

CAESAR DRESSING

3 Combine 2 tablespoons vinegar, lemon juice, garlic and anchovies in a blender or the work bowl of a food processor. Blend until smooth, adding some of the $1/3$ cup olive oil if there isn't enough liquid to move the mixture around.

4 Add the mustard, egg yolk, salt, pepper, Tabasco, Worcestershire and remaining olive oil (if any). Blend until smooth and creamy. Taste for seasoning. If too tangy, add a splash or two of olive oil.

SALAD

5 Divide lettuce among chilled salad plates.

6 Pour dressing over the salad. Add a splash of vinegar and a healthy splash of olive oil. Toss until all leaves are coated.

7 Add croutons and black pepper to taste and toss.

8 Sprinkle with the grated cheese.

9 With a vegetable peeler, shave some of the block of Parmigiano-Reggiano over each serving.

spicy carrot salad

Tagine Dining Gallery, Moroccan, courtesy of Hamid Idrissi

The earthiness of cumin, the pungency of garlic cloves and the sweetness of carrots unite in this simple, refreshing classic Moroccan salad.

SERVES 4–6

2 pounds large carrots, peeled and cut lengthwise into $1/4$-inch strips
Juice of one lemon
$1/2$ cup white wine vinegar
4 cloves garlic, mashed
2 teaspoons cumin
2 tablespoons cilantro, finely chopped
Salt to taste
Black pepper to taste
Cayenne pepper to taste

1　Steam carrots in a covered steamer rack over boiling water until crisp-tender, about 2 to 3 minutes. Set carrots aside to cool.

2　Combine remaining ingredients.

3　When carrots are cool, add to vinegar mixture. Toss well and refrigerate at least 4 hours.

4　Serve at room temperature.

gazala tuna salad

Gazala Place, Druze, courtesy of Gazala Halabi

An abundance of fresh vegetables combine with tuna in this Druze salad to create a colorful and refreshing dish. Its versatility lends itself to a salad, a meze or a main course.

SERVES 4–6

2 medium tomatoes, cut in $1/2$-inch dice
2 small dill pickles, cut in $1/2$-inch dice
2 radishes, cut in $1/4$-inch dice
1 scallion, cut in $1/4$-inch slices
$1/2$ head iceberg lettuce, torn
$1/2$ medium red onion, cut in $1/2$-inch dice
$1/2$ medium red bell pepper, cut in $1/2$-inch dice

3 (6-ounce) cans tuna in oil, drained
Salt and pepper to taste

Juice of $1/2$ lemon
1–2 tablespoons extra virgin olive oil

GARNISH
4 hard-boiled eggs, quartered

1 Place all vegetables in a large mixing bowl.

2 Fold in drained tuna and season with salt and pepper.

3 Spread on a decorative platter. Drizzle with lemon juice and olive oil.

GARNISH
4 Arrange hard-boiled eggs on top.

SPECIALS

Grilled Salmon &
Vegetable Soup
$10.50

Red Pepper
Fettuccini w/
grilled chicken,
red onions & tomatoes
tossed in sesame
oil $18.50

Crispy Atlantic
Salmon w/red pepper
sauce, mashed + vegg
$21-

POULTRY & GAME

I came to New York from Panama at 14 when my mother got a job as a live-in maid and cook. She worked all week and we saw her only on weekends. But she made sure my seven brothers and I learned how to cook and clean. After 45 years, I'm still living and working in Hell's Kitchen and I thank my mother every day. Because of her, I'm lucky to say I have *no* regrets.

—Alberto "Panama" Ellis
Rudy's Bar & Grill

pollo guajira

Guantanamero, Cuban, courtesy of Arnoldo Gonzalez

"Peasant" or "farmer" chicken stuffed with tropical plantains and baked with vegetables in a chicken gravy is a tribute to the home cooking of the Cuban people.

SERVES 4

4 (6–8 ounce) boneless, skinless chicken breasts
2 ripe yellow plantains, sliced lengthwise and cut in half
8 ($1/2$-inch) slices mozzarella cheese
8 toothpicks

$3/4$ cup olive oil
Salt and pepper to season
3 cloves garlic, finely chopped
2 green bell peppers, thinly sliced
2 red bell peppers, thinly sliced
1 medium zucchini, julienned
1 yellow onion, thinly sliced

$1/2$ cup white wine
1 (14-ounce) can chicken gravy
1 cup chicken stock
2 tablespoons tomato sauce
1 teaspoon dried oregano

GARNISH
Parsley

1 Pound chicken breasts to $1/2$ inch thickness. In the middle of each breast, place 2 plantain slices and a slice of cheese.

2 Fold the outside ends of each breast to the middle of breast, forming a ball, and secure each breast with 2 toothpicks.

3 In a large heavy skillet, heat olive oil over medium-high heat. Season each chicken "ball" with salt and pepper; add to skillet and brown on both sides. Remove chicken from skillet and keep warm.

4 Add garlic, bell pepper, zucchini and onion to skillet and sauté 3 to 4 minutes over medium heat.

5 Deglaze the pan with the wine. Stir in gravy, stock, tomato sauce and oregano and blend well.

6 Return chicken to the pan and coat with sauce.

7 Bake in a preheated 400-degree-F oven 30 to 35 minutes, basting occasionally.

GARNISH
8 Sprinkle with parsley and serve immediately.

north african cornish hens

Tagine Dining Gallery, Moroccan, courtesy of Hamid Idrissi

Stuffed with potatoes and Moroccan charmoula, Cornish hens are baked and basted with plain yogurt in the final cooking to bring the exotic into your kitchen.

SERVES 4

3 medium russet potatoes, peeled and cut into
   1-inch chunks
1/2 cup Charmoula marinade (see page 148)
4 (1–1 1/2 pound) Cornish hens
3 tablespoons olive oil
Salt and pepper to season
1 cup plain yogurt

1 In a large saucepan, cover potatoes by 1 inch of water. Bring to a boil and then reduce to a simmer. Cook potatoes until tender, about 15 to 20 minutes.

2 Slightly smash potatoes and blend in Charmoula. Set aside and keep warm.

3 Rinse Cornish hens and pat dry with paper towels. Brush lightly with olive oil and season with salt and pepper.

4 Bake in a preheated 350-degree-F oven for 30 minutes.

5 Remove from oven and stuff each hen with approximately 1/2 cup potato mixture.

6 Return to oven and bake an additional 15 to 20 minutes. (Hens are done when meat thermometer registers 180 degrees in thickest part of the thigh.)

7 Remove from oven and raise temperature to 400 degrees F. Baste hens with yogurt, return to oven and bake an additional 5 to 7 minutes.

8 Allow hens to sit for 10 minutes before serving.

rabbit oreganato

Uncle Nick's Greek Cuisine, Greek, courtesy of
Antonio Manatakis

More flavorful and delicate than chicken,
this Greek-style rabbit is cooked with the
classic Mediterranean ingredients of olive
oil, garlic and lemon. These fresh flavors
are further enhanced by the use of Greek
oregano, which is lighter and fruitier than
other oregano.

SERVES 6

2 rabbits (5–6 pounds total), cut into serving
   pieces
3/4 cup extra virgin olive oil
8 cloves garlic, finely chopped
1/2 medium onion, chopped
Juice of 4–5 lemons
3/4 cup chicken stock
1 tablespoon dried Greek oregano
Salt and pepper to taste

1 Wash rabbit pieces and pat dry with
paper towels.

2 Heat the olive oil in a large heavy pot.
When hot, add garlic and onion and lightly
brown.

3 Add lemon juice, chicken stock and rabbit.

4 Cover pot and simmer about 11/2 hours,
occasionally checking the liquid in pot.
Do not let it dry out. If too dry, add a small
amount of additional stock.

5 When cooked, add oregano and salt and
pepper to taste. Simmer 2 to 3 minutes.

6 Serve immediately.

maria's chicken ipanema

Rice 'n' Beans, Brazilian, courtesy of Maria Lemos

An easy-to-make Brazilian meal using only the freshest of ingredients, including clarified butter, is complete with a crisp green salad and a loaf of Portuguese bread.

SERVES 4

4 (4–6 ounce) boneless, skinless chicken breasts
Salt and pepper to season
3 tablespoons clarified butter
1 tablespoon crushed and minced garlic
1 cup chicken stock
2 plum tomatoes, sliced

GARNISH
1 tablespoon coarsely chopped fresh dill

1 With meat mallet, pound chicken breasts to $1/2$ inch thickness. Season with salt and pepper.

2 In a large heavy skillet, over medium-high heat, heat butter until it begins to sizzle.

3 Add chicken and garlic to skillet and sauté until golden brown, about 2 minutes for each side. (Do not allow butter and garlic to burn.)

4 Deglaze skillet with chicken stock. Reduce heat to medium.

5 Place tomatoes on top of chicken breasts. Cover and cook 1 to 2 minutes to heat tomatoes through. Adjust seasoning.

GARNISH

6 Plate and sprinkle with fresh dill.

chicken tikka masala

Bombay Eats, Indian, courtesy of Prakash Hundalani

This dish of baked marinated cubes ("tikka") of chicken in a luscious curry masala sauce is one of India's favorite meals, with its abundance of exotic spices.

SERVES 4

2 pounds boneless, skinless chicken breasts

MARINADE
4 tablespoons vegetable oil
3 tablespoons fresh lemon juice
3 teaspoons minced ginger
3 teaspoons crushed garlic
$1/4$ cup plain yogurt
$1/4$ teaspoon EACH: white pepper, cumin, nutmeg, ground green cardamom, chili powder and turmeric

Melted butter for basting

CURRY MASALA SAUCE
2 pounds chopped tomatoes
$1 1/4$ cups canned tomato puree
$1/2$ cup plus 2 tablespoons tomato paste
2–3 green chiles, seeded
1 tablespoon red chili powder
2 teaspoons minced fresh gingerroot
1 teaspoon minced garlic
8 green cardamom pods, seeded
4 cups water

$2/3$ cup heavy cream
3 tablespoons butter
Salt to taste
Honey to taste

2 teaspoons julienned ginger
1 teaspoon fenugreek

1 Cut chicken into 1-inch cubes.

MARINADE
2 Combine marinade ingredients and marinate chicken cubes overnight in the refrigerator.

3 Spread out chicken on a baking sheet and bake in preheated 350-degree-F oven 7 to 10 minutes, basting with butter 2 to 3 times.

4 Drain any excess liquid and bake the chicken an additional 2 to 3 minutes.

CURRY MASALA SAUCE
5 In a large Dutch oven, combine the tomatoes, puree, tomato paste, chiles, chili powder, minced ginger, garlic and cardamom. Add 4 cups water.

6 Bring to a boil and immediately reduce heat and simmer, stirring often, 10 to 15 minutes, until the sauce thickens. Strain, return to pot and bring to a boil.

7 Reduce heat to low and stir in heavy cream and butter. Add salt to taste. If sauce is slightly sour, add honey to taste.

8 Fold in chicken cubes, julienned ginger and fenugreek.

9 Serve immediately.

spiced grilled chicken with cherry tomato salad

Zanzibar, African, courtesy of Raul Bravo

African-spiced and marinated chicken breasts are grilled and served with a sweet-and-sour-dressed tomato salad.

SERVES 4

MARINADE
1 cup plain yogurt
1 1/2 teaspoons turmeric powder
1 1/2 teaspoons cumin powder
1 1/2 teaspoons Cajun spice powder
3 tablespoons poultry seasoning
2 tablespoons chili oil

4 (6–8 ounce) boneless, skinless chicken breasts

CHERRY TOMATO SALAD
1 teaspoon sugar
2 teaspoons rice wine vinegar
2 teaspoons olive oil
1 teaspoon thyme
1 1/2 cups cherry tomatoes, cut in half
1/2 pound feta cheese
Cilantro leaves for garnish

SPICED SALT FOR DUSTING
2 teaspoons turmeric powder
2 teaspoons cumin powder
2 teaspoons Creole Spice powder
6 tablespoons poultry seasoning

MARINADE

1 Combine all ingredients in a glass bowl and marinate the chicken for 1 hour.

CHERRY TOMATO SALAD

2 Dissolve the sugar in the vinegar and then add the remaining ingredients.

3 Marinate the tomatoes for 30 minutes.

4 Remove chicken from marinade and grill on stovetop on medium-high heat about 3 to 4 minutes per side.

SPICED SALT

5 Combine all ingredients.

TO SERVE

6 Slice chicken breasts and fan next to Cherry Tomato Salad.

7 Crumble feta cheese over salad. Garnish with cilantro leaves and dust with spiced salt before serving.

squab alla piemontese

Barbetta, Italian, courtesy of Team De Cuisine

Succulent young pigeons are cooked with vegetables and white wine and roasted in the oven for a rich and delicious Italian eating adventure. Only fresh squab can be used, as frozen squab will not produce the same results. Quail can be substituted, but allow 2 per person.

SERVES 4

4 (1¼ pound) fresh (not frozen) squabs, deboned
Salt and pepper to season

4 celery hearts
4 medium yellow onions
4 medium carrots
2 medium leeks
2 tablespoons olive oil
2 tablespoons butter

1 cup dry white wine
6 bay leaves
6 sage leaves
2 sprigs rosemary

1 cup chicken stock, divided

BARBETTA

ESTABLISHED in 1906 in the Maioglio/Astor Townhouse, this restaurant is the oldest Italian restaurant in NYC and the oldest restaurant in the Theater District area. Barbetta is still owned by the founder's daughter, Laura Maioglio. Authentic Piemonte cuisine is served in this elegantly decorated landmark and is a favorite of locals and theatergoers. The family even owns truffle hounds in Italy to sniff out white truffles to be shipped to the restaurant.

1 Clean squab, cut off wings (DO NOT DISCARD), season birds with salt and pepper and truss.

2 Prepare vegetables: wash and dry celery hearts and cut into 1-inch dice. Peel and cut onions into 1-inch dice. Peel and cut carrots into 1-inch dice. Remove green stems from leeks; wash and dry the white part and cut into 1-inch dice.

3 Heat olive oil and butter in a large, heavy, ovenproof saucepan over high heat.

4 Place squabs and wings in saucepan and brown 3 to 4 minutes.

5 Add vegetables to saucepan and brown 4 to 5 minutes.

6 Add the wine and herbs and cook until wine reduces, 4 to 5 minutes.

7 When wine reduces, add ½ cup chicken stock and bring to a boil.

8 Cover saucepan and place in a preheated 350-degree-F oven for 40 to 45 minutes, using remaining stock to baste squabs every 10 to 15 minutes.

9 When birds are done, remove and discard wings. Spoon off any excess fat from sauce.

10 Divide vegetables on 4 plates and place 1 squab on top. Spoon sauce over each.

arroz con pollo criollo
Guantanamero, Cuban, courtesy of Isaias Ortiz

Cuban chicken and rice, cooked in the Caribbean Creole style, is truly a casual get-together event. A one-pot dish of chicken, rice and vegetables seasoned to perfection is taken higher with the addition of white wine and beer.

SERVES 10–12

4 (6–8 ounce) boneless, skinless chicken breasts
1 yellow onion, peeled and quartered
1 bay leaf
1 teaspoon salt

2 tablespoons olive oil
2 cloves garlic, minced
1 large yellow onion, finely chopped
1 green bell pepper, finely chopped

4 cups water
1 cup white wine
1/2 cup canned tomato sauce
2 bay leaves
1/2 teaspoon salt
1/2 teaspoon ground cumin
1/2 teaspoon dried oregano
1/2 teaspoon saffron

5 cups long-grain rice

12 ounces beer
3 roasted red bell peppers, diced
1 cup frozen sweet peas
1 cup frozen diced carrots

1/4 cup extra-virgin olive oil

1 Place chicken, onion, bay leaf and 1 teaspoon salt in a Dutch oven and cover with water by 2 inches. Boil 8 to 12 minutes, until chicken is cooked through.

2 Remove and set aside until cool. When cool, shred chicken into bite-size pieces.

3 In a Dutch oven, heat 2 tablespoons olive oil over high heat. Add garlic, onion and bell pepper and sauté 3 to 4 minutes.

4 Add water, wine and tomato sauce and bring to a boil over medium heat.

5 Stir in the bay leaves, salt, cumin, oregano and saffron and heat 30 seconds.

6 Add rice and continue to cook over medium heat, uncovered, until the rice absorbs most of the liquid, about 15 to 20 minutes.

7 Add the beer, roasted peppers, peas, carrots and shredded chicken.

8 Cook, covered, about 20 minutes, until rice is tender.

9 Remove from heat, fold in olive oil and let stand 10 minutes before serving.

doro wat

Queen of Sheba, Ethiopian, courtesy of Philipos Mengistu

In this high-holiday Ethiopian stew, chicken is slow cooked in a red pepper and spice seasoning and purified butter with hard-boiled eggs. Forks and knives are replaced here by sauce-absorbing injera bread and fingers.

SERVES 4

1 (3–4 pound) skinless chicken, cut up
1 lemon, quartered

4 cups red onion, chopped
1 tablespoon finely chopped garlic
1 tablespoon finely chopped fresh ginger
1 tablespoon ground cardamom
$1/2$ cup Berbere (recipe follows)
2 cups Nitre Kibe (recipe follows)
Salt to taste
6 hard-boiled eggs

1 recipe Injera bread (see page 119)

BERBERE (ETHIOPIAN HOT PEPPER SEASONING) YIELDS $3^1/4$ CUPS
1 teaspoon ground ginger
$1/2$ teaspoon ground cardamom
$1/2$ teaspoon ground coriander
$1/2$ teaspoon ground fenugreek
$1/4$ teaspoon ground cloves

2 cups paprika
$1^1/4$ cups cayenne pepper
1 tablespoon salt
1 teaspoon ground black pepper

1 Rub chicken pieces with lemon.

2 In a large heavy pot on low heat, cook onion, garlic, ginger and cardamom for 20 minutes, stirring frequently to avoid burning. Add small amounts of water as needed to prevent sticking. Add Berbere and continue to cook for 20 minutes, stirring frequently. Add the Nitre Kibe and cook an additional 10 minutes.

3 Put chicken in the pot and cook 15 to 20 minutes, adding water to achieve a stew consistency. Gently stir so as not to remove chicken from the bones and cook for 15 minutes.

4 Season with salt and add whole hard-boiled eggs to the sauce. Simmer 15 to 20 minutes over low heat, until chicken is cooked through.

5 Serve with injera (Ethiopian fermented bread).

BERBERE SEASONING

6 In a large heavy skillet, toast the first 5 ingredients over low heat for 6 to 8 minutes, shaking the skillet or stirring constantly to avoid burning.

7 Add remaining ingredients and continue toasting an additional 10 to 12 minutes, stirring constantly.

8 Cool and store in an airtight container.

NOTE: Recipe can be halved.

NITRE KIBE (ETHIOPIAN PURIFIED BUTTER)
MAKES 3 CUPS
2 pounds unsalted butter
3 whole cloves
2 garlic cloves, smashed
1 cinnamon stick
1 teaspoon peeled and minced fresh ginger
$^1/_2$ teaspoon ground cardamom
$^1/_4$ teaspoon ground fenugreek

INTERNATIONAL GROCERY

THIS small, seventy-year-old grocery is packed from floor to ceiling with culinary delights from every corner of the world. Barrels of brilliant and aromatic spices, legumes and flours crowd the store. The butcher cut pepper is to die for.

NITRE KIBE

9 In a large heavy skillet, melt butter over medium heat and slowly bring to a bubbling stage. Be careful to avoid burning.

10 Add the remaining ingredients; reduce heat to low and simmer, uncovered and undisturbed, for 30 to 40 minutes.

11 When the surface becomes transparent and the milk solids fall to the bottom, strain through cheesecloth. Discard spices and milk solids.

12 Butter will keep in an airtight container at room temperature for 2 months.

NOTE: **Recipe can be halved.**

pollo limone

Becco, Italian, courtesy of Bill Gallagher

Light, refreshing lemony chicken breasts are stuffed with a bread crumb stuffing and baked in a white wine sauce in this classic Italian meal.

SERVES 4

4 (6–8 ounce) boneless, skinless chicken breasts
$^1/_2$ cup fine, dry bread crumbs
$^1/_4$ cup extra virgin olive oil, divided
$^1/_4$ cup chopped fresh parsley, divided
1$^1/_2$ teaspoons dried oregano, divided
Salt to taste
8 toothpicks

1 cup dry white wine
$^1/_2$ cup chicken stock (homemade or canned, reduced sodium)
$^1/_4$ cup fresh lemon juice
1 teaspoon crushed hot red pepper
4 cloves garlic, peeled

1 Cut each chicken breast in half crosswise on a diagonal, yielding two pieces of similar size.

2 Place 2 pieces at a time between two sheets of plastic wrap. With a meat mallet, gently pound chicken to $^1/_2$ inch thickness.

3 In a bowl, toss the bread crumbs, 1 tablespoon olive oil, 1 tablespoon parsley, $^1/_2$ teaspoon oregano and salt to taste until blended.

4 Spread 1 tablespoon bread crumb mixture on each chicken piece, reserving the remaining crumb mixture.

5 Roll each chicken piece into a compact shape with the bread crumb mixture running in a spiral through the center. Secure each roll with 2 toothpicks.

6 Arrange the chicken rolls side by side in a 9-x-13-inch flameproof baking dish, leaving space between the chicken pieces.

7 In a small bowl, combine the wine, chicken stock, lemon juice, hot pepper, the remaining 3 tablespoons olive oil, 1 tablespoon parsley, the remaining 1 teaspoon oregano and salt to taste. Pour into the baking dish.

8 With the side of a chef's knife, flatten the garlic cloves and scatter them around the chicken rolls.

9 Bake in a preheated 475-degree-F oven for 10 minutes.

10 Top the chicken with the remaining bread crumb mixture.

11 Return to the oven and bake until bread topping is golden brown, about 5 minutes.

12 Place the flameproof baking dish directly over medium-high heat. Add the remaining 2 tablespoons parsley and bring the pan juices to a boil. Boil until slightly thickened, about 1 to 2 minutes.

13 Using a slotted spoon, gently transfer the chicken rolls to plates. Remove toothpicks, being careful not to loosen the bread crumb topping.

14 Pour the sauce around, *not over*, the chicken.

15 Serve immediately.

grandmother's chicken patties

Uncle Vanya Cafe, Russian, courtesy of Marina Troshina

Ground chicken "burgers" are breaded and fried in combined oil and butter until golden brown. They are garnished with fresh dill and served with sour cream, typical in Russian cuisine.

SERVES 4

2 pounds boneless, skinless chicken breasts
6 tablespoons butter
2 tablespoons fresh dill
1/8 teaspoon nutmeg
Salt and pepper to taste

2 cups flour
2 eggs, slightly beaten
2 cups fresh bread crumbs

6 tablespoons vegetable oil
6 tablespoons butter

GARNISH
Fresh dill for garnish
Sour cream

1 Cut chicken in 1-inch chunks and place in the work bowl of a food processor with 6 tablespoons butter, dill, nutmeg, salt and pepper.

2 Process until chicken is ground and butter is incorporated. (Do not overprocess.)

3 Chill until very cold.

4 Using 1/2 cup mixture for each patty, form into 3/4-to-1-inch-thick patties.

5 Chill again before frying to maintain the shape of the patties.

6 Coat each patty with flour, dip in egg and coat with bread crumbs.

7 In a large heavy skillet, heat oil and butter over medium-high heat.

8 Fry patties, in batches, for 4 to 5 minutes on each side until brown and crispy. (Add more butter and oil to the skillet if necessary.)

GARNISH

9 Garnish with fresh dill and serve immediately with sour cream.

crispy moulard duck breasts with potato and root vegetable puree

Le Madeleine, Modern French, courtesy of Fabian Pauta

Moulard ducks, bred for foie gras, are dark and meaty. The breasts of these ducks are called magrets. Cooked in a red concord grape sauce and placed on a bed of vegetable puree, the duck becomes the perfect bistro meal.

SERVES 4

POTATO AND ROOT VEGETABLE PUREE
1 large baking potato, peeled and coarsely diced
1 parsnip, peeled and cut into 2-inch pieces
1 turnip, peeled and coarsely diced
$1/2$ cup heavy cream
$1/2$ pound unsalted butter, softened
Salt and pepper to taste

DUCK
1 tablespoon olive oil
4 boneless duck breasts, skin on
Salt and pepper
1 pound red concord grapes, rinsed
1 tablespoon sugar
$1/2$ cup water
Salt and pepper to season
1 tablespoon butter

ROOT VEGETABLE PUREE

1 Boil potato, parsnip and turnip until tender. Puree in a food mill or ricer.

2 In a heavy saucepan, boil milk and cream.

3 Add the puree and whisk to blend.

4 Mix in butter and season with salt and pepper.

DUCK

5 In a large heavy skillet, heat the olive oil.

6 Season duck breasts with salt and pepper and place in hot skillet.

7 Sear skin side down until skin is very crispy, about 5 minutes for medium-rare. For medium-well, turn duck breast and cook an additional 2 to 3 minutes.

8 Remove from pan and set aside.

9 In the same pan, add the grapes, sugar and water and boil until the grapes fall apart.

10 Reduce sauce by half, to about $1/2$ cup.

11 Strain, season with salt and pepper, and whisk in the butter.

12 Slice duck.

TO PLATE

13 Divide puree in the middle of four plates. Place one sliced duck breast on top of puree.

14 Drizzle 2 tablespoons of grape reduction over the duck serving.

fajitas con pollo

El Azteca, Mexican, courtesy of Maria Dias

Fajitas originated with Hispanic ranch hands in Texas in the 1930s. They rapidly spread throughout the country, becoming a popular Mexican favorite. While they were first made with steak, this version uses lighter, healthier chicken.

SERVES 4

CHICKEN

2 pounds boneless, skinless chicken breasts

1/4 cup fresh lemon juice
3 tablespoons minced garlic cloves
Salt and pepper to taste

$1/4$ cup corn oil
$1/4$ cup white wine
2 green bell peppers, seeded and sliced thin
1 red bell pepper, seeded and sliced thin
1 large yellow onion, sliced thin

12 (6-inch) flour tortillas

ACCOMPANIMENTS

Shredded iceberg lettuce, chopped tomatoes, chopped red onion, sour cream and Guacamole (recipe below)

GUACAMOLE

2 Hass avocados, pitted
$1/4$ cup finely chopped tomato
$1/4$ cup finely chopped onion
1 jalapeño, stemmed, seeded and minced
Juice of 1 lime
1 tablespoon corn oil
1 teaspoon finely chopped cilantro
$1/2$ teaspoon minced garlic
Salt and Tabasco Sauce to taste

CHICKEN

1 Cut chicken into $1/2$-inch strips.

2 In a nonreactive bowl, combine lemon juice, garlic, salt and pepper. Add chicken and marinate for 30 minutes. Mix every 10 minutes to coat chicken strips.

3 Remove chicken from marinade and pat dry with paper towels.

4 In a large heavy skillet, heat corn oil over medium-high heat. When hot, sauté chicken until cooked through and browned, 6 to 8 minutes. (Add a little water, if needed, to prevent sticking.)

5 Add wine, bell peppers and onion and cook 3 to 4 minutes.

HEAT TORTILLAS

Microwave Method: Wrap tortillas in plastic wrap and heat on high for 1 to 2 minutes.

Oven Method: Preheat oven to 350 degrees F. Wrap tortillas in foil and bake for 8 to 10 minutes.

Stovetop Method: In an ungreased skillet over medium-high heat, heat tortillas (one at a time) until warm, 10 to 15 seconds on each side.

GUACAMOLE

6 Remove pulp from avocado with a spoon.

7 Add remaining ingredients and mash to a creamy consistency.

TO SERVE

8 Place chicken on a platter and surround with bowls of accompaniments.

Farouj Mashwi

La Kabbr, Middle Eastern, courtesy of Farouk Mansoor

In this Iraqi preparation, Cornish hens are split and marinated in a simple yet flavorful marinade and baked until the delicate skin is crisp and golden brown. Serve with couscous and an Iraqi salad for an exotic getaway.

SERVES 4

MARINADE
2–3 tablespoons olive oil
1 teaspoon granulated garlic
1/2 teaspoon dried rosemary
Juice of 1 lemon

CHICKEN
4 (1 1/2 pound) Cornish hens, split in half
Salt and pepper to taste

MARINADE

1 Whisk together the olive oil, garlic, rosemary and lemon juice.

2 Rinse and dry the Cornish hens and season with salt and pepper.

3 Place in a nonreactive dish and pour marinade over hens, coating well.

4 Marinate 1 hour at room temperature.

CHICKEN

5 Place in a lightly oiled baking pan and bake in a preheated 350-degree-F oven for 30 to 40 minutes, or until the thickest part of thighs registers 170 degrees F.

tequila chicken quesadillas

Hudson Yards Cafe, Traditional American, courtesy of Jimmy Reardon

The kick that elevates these quesadillas is tequila. Chicken, bell peppers and onion are sautéed and simmered in the liquor to absorb a unique—and appropriate—flavor.

SERVES 4

1/2 cup olive oil
2 pounds boneless, skinless chicken breasts, cut into thin strips
1 green bell pepper, thinly sliced
1 red bell pepper, thinly sliced
1 medium yellow onion, thinly sliced
1/2 cup tequila
Salt and pepper to taste

Olive oil to brush on pan
6 (8-inch) flour tortillas

1 cup shredded Monterey Jack cheese

1 Hass avocado, peeled and sliced
1 cup sour cream

1 In a large heavy skillet, heat 1/2 cup olive oil over medium-high heat. Add chicken strips, bell peppers, onion and tequila.

2 Reduce heat to medium and sauté until vegetables are translucent.

3 Season with salt and pepper and simmer over medium-low heat for 15 minutes.

4 Brush a 10-inch skillet with olive oil and heat over medium-high heat.

5 Place a tortilla in the skillet and cook until light brown on one side, about 1 minute.

6 Spread one-third of the chicken-vegetable mixture on a tortilla, sprinkle with cheese and cook on low until cheese melts, about 2 minutes.

7 Place another tortilla on top and, with a spatula, carefully flip the quesadilla and cook an additional 1 to 2 minutes.

8 Cook the remaining 2 quesadillas in the same manner.

9 Cut each quesadilla in quarters and top with avocado and sour cream.

10 Serve immediately, three wedges per person.

Working at an Irish pub and restaurant on the Hudson River in Hell's Kitchen is a new adventure every day. The commercial ships and cruise ships provide a constant flow of river traffic and give the area its strong international flavor. And Manhattan's Circle Line and the *Intrepid* bring in 800,000 tourists a year. On a typical day at work, I may hear as many as 10 different languages. Guess you can say I can travel the world and know how to order food and drink like a local. And isn't that what it's all about!

—Frankie Ford
P. D. O'Hurley's

hell's kitchen horseradish burger

Smith's Bar, Irish, courtesy of Jim Hanley

Commonly served with beef on the side, here horseradish is mixed into the meat before cooking, giving a pungent zing to these burgers.

SERVES 4

2 pounds ground beef
Salt and pepper to taste
2 cups prepared horseradish, divided
$1/2$ cup mayonnaise
4 brioche hamburger rolls with sesame seeds
4 lettuce leaves
4 slices tomato
4 slices red onion

1 Season ground beef with salt and pepper and mix in $1^1/2$ cups horseradish. Form into 4 patties.

2 Mix $1/2$ cup mayonnaise with $1/2$ cup horseradish.

3 Grill burgers 4 minutes per side for medium, 1 to 2 minutes more for well-done.

4 Toast rolls under broiler about 1 minute, until golden brown.

5 Spread horseradish mayo on rolls. Place lettuce, tomato, and onion on roll.

6 Add burger and serve with a side of fries.

ESPOSITO'S PORK SHOP

IN operation since 1890, this family-owned business is well known for its pork; but it purveys all manner of meats. In addition to beef, lamb and veal, it also supplies oxtail, quail and pheasant, and pig's ears, toes and heads. True to old-world tradition, nothing is wasted in this nearly 120-year-old butcher shop. Esposito's also provides tips on preparation. And their luscious specialty sausage? Four to six thousand pounds are sold daily.

andouille smothered in black-eyed peas

Delta Grill, Louisiana Cuisine, courtesy of Ignacio Castillo

This most popular Cajun smoked pork sausage employs one of Louisiana's favorite cooking methods—smothering, or étouffée.

SERVES 6

1/4 cup vegetable oil
2 cups diced celery
1 cup diced green pepper
2 cups diced onion
3 cloves garlic, finely chopped
2 tablespoons finely chopped chipotle peppers
2 tablespoons Delta Grill Cajun Seasoning
Salt and pepper to taste

1 (16-ounce) bag dried black-eyed peas
2 quarts (8 cups) chicken stock
1 pound andouille sausage
2 tablespoons unsalted butter

Cooked white rice

1 **In a 4-quart pot, heat oil over medium heat.**

2 **Combine celery, green pepper, onion, garlic, chipotle peppers, seasoning, and salt and pepper. Add to pot and sauté 7 to 8 minutes.**

3 **Add the black-eyed peas and chicken stock. Bring to a boil; reduce heat and simmer until peas are tender (1 to 1 1/2 hours).**

4 **While peas are cooking, cut andouille diagonally into 1-inch pieces.**

5 **In a large skillet, melt butter until foamy. Add andouille and sauté until browned, 6 to 7 minutes.**

6 **Add browned sausage to cooked black-eyed peas and simmer 5 to 10 minutes.**

7 **Serve with white rice.**

quzi

La Kabbr, Middle Eastern, courtesy of Farouk Mansoor

Middle Eastern–style lamb shanks are boiled for utmost tenderness and then roasted in an oven until richly browned. Serve with rice pilaf, chopped salad and warm pita bread for a delicious, no-fuss meal.

SERVES 4

4 (1-pound) lamb shanks, washed and dried

1 large onion, sliced
1 teaspoon seasoning salt
$1/2$ teaspoon granulated garlic
$1/2$ teaspoon salt

1 Place lamb shanks in a Dutch oven and cover with water by 2 inches. Bring to a boil and cook for 2 hours, adding more water as needed.

2 Drain and pat shanks dry.

3 Place shanks in a large baking pan and layer onion slices on top and sprinkle with seasonings.

4 Bake in a preheated 350-degree-F oven for 15 to 20 minutes, until golden brown.

koenigsberger klopse

Hallo Berlin, German, courtesy of Rolf Babiel

German white meatballs are seasoned with brown mustard and caraway seeds, and then boiled and served with a pickled-caper-and-lemon gravy.

SERVES 6

1 French roll

MEATBALLS
12 ounces ($^3/_4$ pound) ground beef
12 ounces ($^3/_4$ pound) ground pork
2 eggs
1 small onion, chopped
2 tablespoons brown mustard
1$^1/_2$ tablespoons caraway seeds
$^1/_2$ teaspoon granulated garlic
Salt and pepper to taste
6 cups water, salted

PICKLED-CAPER-AND-LEMON GRAVY
3 tablespoons flour
3 tablespoons water
$^1/_4$ cup capers
Juice from 1 lemon
1 teaspoon granulated garlic
Salt and pepper
1 egg, beaten
2 tablespoons butter, optional

Mashed potatoes or noodles

1 Soak French roll in 1 cup water for 10 minutes.

2 In a large bowl, mix beef, pork, eggs, onion, brown mustard, caraway seeds and salt and pepper. And granulated garlic.

3 Remove French roll from water and squeeze dry. Add to meat mixture and combine well.

4 Shape the meat mixture into 2-inch balls.

5 In a large pot, bring water to a boil. Put meatballs in the boiling water, bring back to a boil and reduce heat to low.

6 Cover pot and simmer meatballs 15 to 20 minutes.

7 With a slotted spoon, remove meatballs; set aside and keep warm.

8 Reserve 2 cups of the cooking broth in the pot.

PICKLED-CAPER-AND-LEMON GRAVY

9 Dissolve flour in the water. Stir into the reserved 2 cups broth.

10 Add capers, lemon juice, garlic, and salt and pepper and simmer 7 to 8 minutes.

11 Whisk $^1/_4$ cup broth into the egg to temper, and then stir into the gravy. Stir in the butter, if desired, for a creamier, richer gravy.

12 Put meatballs in gravy and heat over medium-low for 4 to 5 minutes.

13 Serve with mashed potatoes or noodles and a string bean salad.

railroad pork chops with apricot-mango sauce

Hudson Yards Cafe, Traditional American, courtesy of Jimmy Reardon

Succulent marinated pork chops are cooked to perfection and then topped with a pungent apple, dried apricot and mango chutney sauce. A side of your favorite sweet potato dish is the ideal accompaniment to this multiflavored meal.

SERVES 4

MARINADE
1 cup extra-virgin olive oil
1 tablespoon chopped fresh thyme
Salt and pepper

4 (1-inch-thick) center-cut pork chops

APRICOT-MANGO SAUCE
$1/4$ cup extra-virgin olive oil
1 medium red onion, chopped
1 Granny Smith apple cut in $1/2$-inch dice
$1/3$ cup plus 2 tablespoons dried apricots
2 tablespoons mango chutney
2 sprigs fresh rosemary

GARNISH
Fresh rosemary sprigs

MARINADE

1 In a glass dish or nonreactive pan, combine olive oil, thyme, and salt and pepper.

2 Coat pork chops thoroughly and marinate at room temperature for 1 hour.

APRICOT-MANGO SAUCE

3 In a heavy skillet, heat olive oil over medium heat.

4 Add the onion, apple, apricots, chutney and 2 sprigs rosemary; sauté over low heat for 15 minutes.

5 Set aside and keep warm.

TO FINISH THE DISH

6 In a large heavy skillet, heat marinade over medium-high heat.

7 Reduce heat to medium-low and add pork chops. Cook for 7 to 8 minutes, until browned. Turn and cook an additional 6 to 7 minutes to brown opposite side.

8 Remove pork chops, add sauce to skillet and heat 1 to 2 minutes.

9 Plate pork chops and spoon sauce on top.

GARNISH

10 Arrange rosemary sprigs on plates.

yebeg tibs

Queen of Sheba, Ethiopian, courtesy of
Philipos Mengistu

Tibs are sautéed chunks of chicken, beef or lamb. In this Ethiopian stew, lamb is marinated in red wine, sautéed and served on a "tablecloth" of injera—fermented Ethiopian bread. If you want to make your own injera, you need to start it two days ahead.

SERVES 4

2 pounds boneless lamb, cut in 1-inch cube

MARINADE
1 cup red wine
1 large red onion, chopped

$1/2$ cup vegetable oil
1 jalapeño, seeded and finely chopped
1 clove garlic, minced
$1/2$ teaspoon freshly ground black pepper
$1/2$ teaspoon dried rosemary
Salt and pepper to taste

1 Marinate lamb in red wine mixed with onion for 1 hour, stirring every 20 minutes.

2 In a large heavy pot, heat oil over high heat.

3 Add lamb and marinade, jalapeño, garlic, pepper and rosemary.

4 Reduce heat to medium and cook, stirring occasionally, until lamb is cooked, 6 to 8 minutes. Add a small amount of water as needed to avoid sticking.

5 Season with salt and pepper.

6 Serve with Injera.

injera

YIELDS 6–8 ROUNDS

2 cups teff*
6 cups warm water, divided
$1/2$ cup all-purpose flour

1 In bowl, mix teff with $4 1/2$ cups warm water.

2 In a separate bowl, mix the flour with the remaining $1 1/2$ cups warm water.

3 Set both bowls aside at room temperature for three days to allow fermentation to take place. (Bubbles will appear.)

4 On the third night, combine teff and flour mixes and let stand overnight. Cook the following morning.

5 Heat a 12-inch nonstick or cast-iron skillet over medium heat.

6 Ladle in a generous $1/4$ cup of mix and swirl, as if making a crepe, but cook on only one side until small holes appear. Remove injera carefully and set aside to cool.

* Teff are tiny round khaki-colored grains that create an airy, bubbly bread. Teff can be purchased in African markets. Injera can also be purchased in African markets or ordered online.

spiha

Gazala Place, Druze, courtesy of Gazala Halabi

In this Middle Eastern favorite, phyllo pockets are filled with beef, lamb, pine nuts and spice and then baked. The pockets can be made smaller and served as appetizers.

SERVES 4

2 tablespoons olive oil
2 cloves garlic, minced
1 medium onion, chopped

$1/4$ pound ground beef
$1/4$ pound ground lamb
2 tablespoons pine nuts
$1/2$ teaspoon allspice
Salt and pepper to taste

2 sheets frozen phyllo, thawed
$1/4$ cup melted unsalted butter

1 In a large heavy skillet, heat olive oil over medium-high heat.

2 Add garlic and onion, reduce heat to medium, and cook 2 to 3 minutes.

3 Stir in beef, lamb, pine nuts, allspice and salt and pepper; mix well.

4 Cover and cook over medium-low heat for 30 to 35 minutes, stirring frequently to avoid sticking.

5 Drain and keep warm.

6 Grease a baking sheet with a little melted butter.

7 Cut each phyllo sheet into 4 equal squares and brush both sides with butter.

8 Place 4 squares on the baking sheet.

9 Evenly divide the meat mixture in the center of the four squares.

10 Cover filled squares with the remaining 4 squares and seal edges to enclose the "pockets."

11 Brush lightly with butter and bake in a 350-degree-F preheated oven until golden and crisp, about 10 to 12 minutes.

spiedino macelleria

Cascina Ristorante, Italian, courtesy of Gualtiero Carosi

Italian "butcher shop" skewers offer the best of everything—a succulent assortment of meats, marinated and roasted to perfection, with a red wine reduction.

SERVES 4

2 sweet Italian sausages (8–10 ounces total), each cut into 4 pieces
8 (1-inch) cubes beef tenderloin (8–10 ounces total)
8 (1-inch) cubes pork tenderloin (8–10 ounces total)
4 (1-inch) cubes pancetta (4–5 ounces total)

Olive oil to coat meat
2 cloves garlic, sliced
1/4 teaspoon dried rosemary
Pepper to taste
2 cups Barolo (or any full-bodied red wine)
Salt and freshly ground black pepper to taste

4 wooden skewers (soaked in water for about 1 hour)
8 ounces mixed salad greens
Extra virgin olive oil

1 In a large bowl, coat meats with olive oil, garlic, rosemary and pepper. Marinate in the refrigerator for 6 hours, stirring occasionally.

2 Divide meat cubes evenly onto four presoaked 12-inch wooden skewers.

3 Place skewers in a 9 x 13-inch baking dish and pour wine over the meat.

4 Sprinkle with salt and pepper and cook in a preheated 375-degree-F oven about 10 to 15 minutes, until the wine evaporates to a thick sauce and the meat is brown and crispy.

5 Divide the salad greens onto four cold plates and place 1 skewer on top.

6 Distribute the wine reduction on top of the four dishes.

7 Drizzle with extra-virgin olive oil and serve.

RUDY'S BAR & GRILLE

RUDY'S is proud to say that it is a Hell's Kitchen institution that's been open legally for seventy-five years. Baron Von Swine, a six-foot pig outside the entrance, welcomes all and is one of the most photographed New York City "landmarks." Free hot dogs are served with a drink purchase.

pepper steak

Mee Noodle, Chinese, courtesy of Harry Sim

Green bell peppers and beef are a classic twosome in Chinese cuisine. Cooked in stock, soy sauce and rice wine, this stir-fry takes on a typical Eastern flavor.

SERVES 4–6

1 pound flank steak, cut in 1-inch strips
2$^1/_2$ teaspoons cornstarch, divided

$^1/_4$ cup vegetable oil
1$^1/_2$ tablespoons freshly grated ginger
1 teaspoon minced garlic
1 green bell pepper, cut in $^1/_2$-inch strips
1 onion, cut in $^1/_2$-inch strips

$^1/_2$ cup beef stock
3 tablespoons soy sauce
2 tablespoons Chinese rice wine*
1 tablespoon sugar
Salt and pepper to taste

1 Place meat in a large bowl and mix in 1–2 tablespoons water and 1 teaspoon cornstarch.

2 In a wok or large heavy skillet, heat oil over high heat.

3 Add ginger and garlic and sauté for 2 minutes.

4 Add beef, pepper and onion and stir-fry for 2 to 3 minutes.

5 Dissolve 1$^1/_2$ teaspoons cornstarch in beef stock. Stir in soy sauce, rice wine and sugar and blend well.

6 Pour stock mixture over beef and peppers and boil, stirring constantly, until sauce thickens.

7 Season with salt and pepper.

8 Serve with white rice.

* Dry sherry can be substituted.

gaeng dang

Olieng, Thai, courtesy of Nid Euashachai

Beef is stir-fried in red curry paste, fish sauce and coconut milk to capture the exotic flavors of the East.

Serves 4

2 tablespoons vegetable oil
2 tablespoons red curry paste
1 cup beef, sliced in strips
1 teaspoon sugar
2 tablespoons fish sauce
2 cups coconut milk
1/2 cup canned bamboo strips
1/4 cup chopped red bell pepper
10 fresh kaffir lime leaves
1/4 cup chopped fresh basil

Cooked rice

1 In a large heavy skillet, heat oil over medium-high heat. Add red curry paste and stir-fry for 1 minute.

2 Add beef, sugar and fish sauce and cook another 1 minute.

3 Stir in coconut milk and bamboo strips and heat until boiling.

4 Add bell pepper, lime leaves, and basil and cook 1 to 2 minutes.

5 Serve with rice.

alexandre kebab

Troy Turkish Grill, Turkish, courtesy of Nurettin Kirbiyic

Served on a large decorative platter, this Turkish meal of lamb placed on a bed of pita, yogurt and tomato sauce is a beautiful, impressive and well-balanced family-style meal.

SERVES 4

MARINADE
3/4 cup olive oil
1/4 cup yogurt
1/2 cup finely chopped onion
1 tablespoon fresh lemon juice
1 teaspoon dried thyme
Salt and pepper

2 pounds lamb, cut into 1 1/2-inch cubes

TOMATO SAUCE
2 tablespoons olive oil
1 cup chopped onion
2 cloves garlic, minced
2 large chile peppers, seeded and chopped
3 large tomatoes, chopped
2 tablespoons tomato paste
1 teaspoon dried thyme
Salt and pepper to taste

YOGURT
2 cups plain yogurt, room temperature
2 cloves garlic, minced

4 (6-inch) pita rounds, cut into 2-inch squares
2 scallions, cut into 1/4-inch pieces

MARINADE

1 Mix marinade ingredients and marinate lamb overnight in the refrigerator.

TOMATO SAUCE

2 In a heavy saucepan, heat olive oil over medium-high heat and sauté onion, garlic and chili peppers about 3 to 4 minutes.

3 Add tomatoes, tomato paste and thyme. Reduce heat and simmer, mashing tomatoes, for 15 to 20 minutes, until sauce forms.

4 Season with salt and pepper and keep warm.

YOGURT

5 Combine yogurt and garlic and set aside in a warm place for the flavors to blend.

TO FINISH THE DISH

6 Thread lamb cubes onto metal or wooden skewers that have been soaked in water for 30 minutes, and season with salt and pepper.

7 Heat a stovetop grill and grill lamb skewers for 2 to 3 minutes on each side, being careful not to overcook.

8 Place pita squares on a large serving platter.

9 Spread with yogurt-garlic mixture.

10 Top the yogurt with tomato sauce, leaving a yogurt border.

11 Remove lamb cubes from skewers and place over sauce.

12 Sprinkle with scallions and serve immediately.

corned beef and cabbage

McQuaid's Public House, Irish, courtesy of Bernadette Hunter

Ireland's hearty, comforting dish brings to mind shamrocks and St. Patrick's Day. It's unlikely there will be leftovers, but, just in case, they make great Reuben sandwiches (recipe below).

SERVES 6–8

1 (5–6 pound) corned beef with spice
   seasoning
2 bay leaves

4–5 large red potatoes, quartered
1 pound baby carrots
1 large onion, quartered
1 medium green cabbage, cut in wedges

Chopped fresh parsley

1 Cut corned beef in half and place in a large Dutch oven.

2 Cover with water by 1 inch and add packaged seasoning and bay leaves.

3 Bring to a boil, reduce heat and simmer for 2 to 3 hours, until meat is tender and a knife easily pierces the beef.

4 Add water as needed to cover beef during the cooking process, and skim any foam that rises to the surface during cooking.

5 When corned beef is done, place in a baking dish, add 1 cup of cooking liquid, cover with aluminum foil and keep warm in a 200-degree-F oven.

6 Add potatoes and carrots to the beef stock and simmer for 8 to 10 minutes.

7 Add the onion and cabbage and continue to simmer for 10 to 12 minutes, until all vegetables are tender. (Do not overcook vegetables.)

8 Plate corned beef on a large platter, surround with vegetables, drizzle with cooking liquid and garnish with parsley.

bernie's leftover reubens

McQuaid's Public House, Irish, courtesy of Bernadette Hunter

YIELDS 1–2 MELTS

4 slices rye bread, toasted
1/2 cup Russian dressing
1 1/2 cups sauerkraut, drained and squeeze-
   dried
1 1/2 cups warm corned beef
4 slices Swiss cheese

1 Spread each piece of bread with 2 tablespoons Russian dressing.

2 Divide sauerkraut among the 4 slices.

3 Top each slice with warm corned beef.

4 Top the corned beef with a slice of cheese.

5 Place under the broiler until cheese melts, 1 to 2 minutes.

SEAFOOD

As a child, I visited New York from Argentina and made the decision that when I was eighteen I would move to Manhattan and open my own restaurant. With a mother from Italy and a father from Spain, I had always been exposed to international foods. Having a passion for the food, music and art of Spain, I wanted a tapas bar with music and a long wall where I could display my paintings. Today I have it in Hell's Kitchen, where I've lived for over 40 years.

—Guillermo Vidal
Cafe Andalucia

fish 'n' chips

P. D. O'Hurley's, Irish, courtesy of Paul Loftus

An Irish pub favorite, beer-battered fish 'n' chips are loved worldwide by both adults and children. The dish is traditionally served with cider vinegar and sprinkled with coarse sea salt.

SERVES 4

Vegetable oil for deep frying

3 large russet potatoes, cut into $1/3$-inch wedges

BEER BATTER
2 cups beer
2 eggs
1 tablespoon baking powder
$1/2$ teaspoon Tabasco Sauce
$1/2$ teaspoon Worcestershire sauce
$1/2$ teaspoon paprika
$2 1/2$ cups flour

4 (8-ounce) cod filets, cut in half

CHIPS

1 Heat 3 inches of oil in a large pot to 375 degrees F.

2 Pat potatoes dry and fry in batches until golden brown. Remove to a baking pan and keep warm in a 200-degree-F oven.

BEER BATTER

3 In a large bowl, mix beer, eggs, baking powder, Tabasco, Worcestershire and paprika until well blended.

4 Gradually whisk in flour until the liquid coats the back of a spoon.

TO FINISH THE DISH

5 With tongs, dip fish in the batter, shake off excess and fry in hot vegetable oil until golden brown and crispy, 5 to 8 minutes. Drain on paper towels.

6 Serve with french fries.

pulpo ajo

Cafe Andalucia, Spanish Tapas, courtesy of Guillermo Vidal

This popular food of Spain is enhanced by the combination of both sweet and hot paprika. While here it is an entree, pulpo can be served as a tapa, one of Spain's "little dishes."

SERVES 4

1 (2–3 pound) octopus, cleaned and rinsed
2 bay leaves
1 teaspoon dried thyme
1 lemon, quartered
3–4 tablespoons extra virgin olive oil
8 cloves garlic, sliced
2 cups white wine
2 tablespoons sweet paprika
1 teaspoon salt
Hot paprika to taste
1/4 cup minced flat-leaf parsley

1 In a stockpot, place octopus, bay leaves, thyme and lemon. Add water to cover. Bring to a boil over high heat. Lower heat and simmer octopus until tender, about 1 to 1^1/$_2$ hours. (Test: knifepoint goes in easily.)

2 Drain octopus and cut into 1-inch pieces.

3 Heat oil in a large heavy skillet. Add octopus and sauté until lightly browned, about 4 to 5 minutes.

4 Add garlic and cook an additional 2 to 3 minutes.

5 Add wine and paprika.

6 Raise heat and bring to a boil.

7 Lower heat and cook until liquid thickens, about 10 to 15 minutes.

8 Season with salt and hot paprika to taste.

9 Garnish with parsley.

pan-fried catfish with red pepper black-eyed pea gravy

B. Smith, Global Eclectic, courtesy of B. Smith

Two southern favorites, sweet catfish and black-eyed peas, marry to produce a delectable and unique "feel-good" dish. Mashed potatoes make an excellent accompaniment.

SERVES 4

4 (8-ounce) catfish fillets
$1/2$ cup yellow cornmeal
$1/4$ cup all-purpose flour
1 teaspoon salt
1 teaspoon Creole seasoning
$1/2$ teaspoon Hungarian hot paprika
$1/4$ teaspoon ground black pepper
$3/4$ cup milk
6 tablespoons unsalted butter or canola oil, divided
Lemon wedges for garnish
$1/4$ cup coarsely chopped flat-leaf parsley

1 recipe Red Pepper Black-Eyed Pea Gravy

1 Rinse the fillets and pat them dry with paper towels.

2 Mix the cornmeal, flour, salt, Creole seasoning, paprika and pepper together in a shallow dish.

3 Pour the milk into a second shallow dish.

4 Dip the fillets into the milk and then into the cornmeal mixture, coating them well and shaking off any excess.

5 Heat half the butter or oil in a skillet over medium heat and fry two of the fillets for 3 to 4 minutes on each side, until the fish flakes easily when tested with a fork.

6 Transfer the fillets to a serving platter and keep warm. Repeat with remaining butter or oil and fillets.

7 Serve immediately, with lemon wedges and a sprinkle of chopped parsley and accompanied by Red Pepper Black-Eyed Pea Gravy (recipe follows).

red pepper black-eyed pea gravy

1 tablespoon vegetable oil
$^1/_2$ cup chopped shallots
3 tablespoons red wine
$^3/_4$ teaspoon Hungarian hot paprika
$^3/_4$ teaspoon Creole seasoning
2 tablespoons clam juice
$^1/_2$ cup chicken stock, divided
1 (15-ounce) can black-eyed peas, rinsed and
  drained
2 bay leaves
2 large red bell peppers, roasted, skin removed
Chopped parsley for garnish

1 In a sauté pan, heat oil over medium heat.

2 Add shallots and sauté for 3 to 4 minutes, until soft.

3 Add wine, paprika and Creole seasoning. Cook a few minutes until the wine has evaporated.

4 Add the clam juice, $^1/_4$ cup chicken stock, black-eyed peas and bay leaves. Bring to a boil and simmer.

5 In a food processor, blend roasted red peppers and remaining $^1/_4$ cup chicken stock.

6 Add to the black-eyed pea mixture and cook 5 minutes longer, stirring occasionally.

7 Remove bay leaves; adjust seasoning to taste.

masgoof

La Kabbr, Middle Eastern, courtesy of Farouk Mansoor

Butterflied whole striped bass are broiled and topped with colorful vegetables in this easy, healthy and beautifully impressive Middle Eastern fish dish.

SERVES 4

4 whole (1¹/2-pound) striped bass
Salt and pepper to taste
Curry powder to taste
Olive oil
1/2 cup white wine
8 (1/2-inch slices) tomato
8 (1/2-inch slices) green bell pepper
8 (1/2-inch slices) onion
8 (1/4-inch slices) lemon

1 Butterfly the fish, leaving the heads on. Season both sides with salt, pepper and curry powder.

2 Leave skin on and make two or three shallow gashes on each fish to prevent curling during broiling.

3 Brush lightly with olive oil and place in a shallow baking pan with wine.

4 Broil 6 inches from broiler for 8 to 10 minutes. Do not overcook or fish will dry out.

5 Remove from oven and place 2 slices of each vegetable and 2 slices lemon on fish.

6 Place under broiler and cook 3 to 4 minutes.

shrimp bhuna

Bombay Eats, Indian, courtesy of Prakash Hundalani

Bhuna is a process of cooking spices in hot oil, and bhuna curry is usually dry and cooked in coconut. Bhuna masala can be purchased in Indian grocery stores and some gourmet shops.

SERVES 4

MARINADE
1/2 cup plain yogurt
2 tablespoons fresh lemon juice
2 teaspoons olive oil
1/2 teaspoon paprika
1/2 teaspoon allspice
1/2 teaspoon curry powder
Salt to taste

SHRIMP
1 pound (20–25 count) shrimp, peeled and deveined

2 tablespoons corn oil
4–6 mushrooms, halved
1 medium onion, thinly sliced
1 medium green bell pepper, thinly sliced
1 tablespoon bhuna masala
1/4 teaspoon minced garlic
Salt and pepper to taste

1 medium tomato, cut into 1/2-inch dice
1 tablespoon chopped fresh cilantro

GARNISH
Freshly chopped cilantro and sliced tomato

MARINADE

1 Mix marinade ingredients; add shrimp and marinate in the refrigerator 3 to 4 hours.

SHRIMP

2 Place shrimp in a single layer in a broiling pan and broil 2 to 3 minutes.

3 Drain and reserve the marinade.

4 In a large heavy skillet, heat corn oil over medium-high heat.

5 Add the mushrooms, onion, bell pepper, bhuna masala, garlic, and salt and pepper.

6 Sauté 3 to 5 minutes, stirring often and adding reserved marinade a spoonful at a time to prevent drying.

7 When vegetables are cooked, fold in the shrimp, tomatoes and cilantro, and cook 2 to 3 minutes.

GARNISH

8 Garnish with chopped cilantro and tomato slices.

pepper-and-almond-crusted tuna steak

Druids, Irish, courtesy of Francisco Velazco

In this tuna dish, almonds are combined with a pepper coating to create a subtle contrast and balance, while the veal stock added to the balsamic reduction intensifies the flavor of the fish.

SERVES 4

1 cup sliced almonds
3 tablespoons coarsely ground black pepper
Zest from 2 lemons
4 (6-ounce) tuna steaks, 1 inch thick
1/4 cup olive oil
1 recipe Balsamic Reduction
2 tablespoons flat-leaf parsley, coarsely chopped

1 Toast almonds in a preheated 350-degree-F oven for 5 to 10 minutes, until golden brown.

2 Cool and grind almonds in the work bowl of a food processor. (Do not overprocess, as you want to avoid it turning into a paste.)

3 Mix almonds with the black pepper and lemon zest. Coat tuna steaks with mixture, pressing so the coating adheres.

4 In a large heavy skillet, heat olive oil over medium-high heat.

5 Reduce heat to medium and carefully add crusted tuna steaks. Cook until coating turns golden brown, about 2 to 3 minutes. With a spatula, carefully turn tuna and cook an additional 2 minutes for rare or 3 minutes for medium-rare.

6 Plate tuna steaks and drizzle Balsamic Reduction (recipe follows) around the tuna steaks.

7 Sprinkle with parsley.

balsamic reduction

2 tablespoons butter
2 shallots, finely chopped
1 1/2 cups balsamic vinegar
1/2 cup veal stock
2 tablespoons Worcestershire sauce
Salt to taste

1 In a heavy saucepan, heat butter over medium heat and sauté shallots until transparent.

2 Add vinegar, veal stock and Worcestershire sauce.

3 Cook over medium heat, stirring constantly until thickened and reduced by half.

4 Adjust salt and pepper. Set aside and keep warm.

shrimp santorini à la tony

Uncle Nick's Greek Cuisine, Greek, courtesy of Antonio Manatakis

Experience the Greek Isles when you indulge in this delicious dish of shrimp, tomatoes and feta.

SERVES 4

$1/2$ cup plus 1 tablespoon olive oil, divided
1 tablespoon minced onion
4 cloves garlic, minced
1 (32-ounce) can pureed tomatoes
$1/2$ cup red wine
3–4 fresh basil leaves
1 small hot pepper, sliced
$1/2$ teaspoon salt
$1/2$ teaspoon pepper
24 large shrimp, peeled and deveined
$1/2$ cup feta cheese, crumbled

1 Heat 1 tablespoon olive oil in a heavy saucepan, and gently sauté the onion and garlic until soft but not brown.

2 Add pureed tomatoes, $1/2$ cup oil and rest of ingredients except the shrimp and feta cheese.

3 Simmer, covered, for 20 minutes, until the tomato sauce thickens.

4 Add shrimp and feta. Simmer for 10 minutes, stirring gently to melt the cheese and cook the shrimp.

5 Serve with rice.

chilean sea bass with coconut curry sauce

Bamboo 52, Japanese, courtesy of Kevin Wunkei Chan

Not related to bass, Chilean sea bass is actually a toothfish. Simply baked with butter, this Japanese dish is napped with an easy-to-make, exotic, room-temperature sauce.

SERVES 4

5 tablespoons unsalted butter, divided
4 (6-ounce) Chilean sea bass fillets
Salt and pepper to taste
2 tablespoons coconut milk
1 tablespoon mayonnaise
1 teaspoon curry powder (more or less, to taste)
1 tablespoon chopped cilantro

1 Preheat oven to 350 degrees F.

2 Grease a baking dish with 1 tablespoon butter.

3 Place fillets in dish and top each with 1 tablespoon butter. Season with salt and pepper.

4 Bake for 20 to 25 minutes.

5 Blend coconut milk, mayonnaise and curry powder well.

6 Plate fish and drizzle with coconut curry sauce.

7 Garnish with cilantro.

pla lad prik

Olieng, Thai, courtesy of Nid Euashachai

A whole snapper is deep-fried to perfection and topped with a delectable Thai sauce. Beautifully presented on a decorative platter in the center of the table, this fish dish is shared by guests.

SERVES 4

SAUCE
2 tablespoons vegetable oil
1 tablespoon chopped garlic
1 tablespoon chili paste
1/4 small onion, sliced
1/4 small bell pepper, sliced
2 tablespoons tamarind juice
1 tablespoon fish sauce (nuoc mam or nam pla)
1 tablespoon sugar
1/4 cup chicken stock

FISH
Vegetable oil for deep frying
1 whole snapper (2–3 pounds), gutted, washed and thoroughly dried
Flour for dredging

GARNISH
1/2 cup fresh basil leaves
1 tablespoon sliced scallion

4 portions cooked rice

SAUCE

1 Heat oil in a large heavy saucepan over medium-high heat. Sauté garlic, chili paste, onion and bell pepper, stirring, for 3 to 4 minutes, until light brown.

2 Stir in tamarind juice, fish sauce, sugar and stock; cook 1 to 2 minutes.

3 Set aside and keep warm.

FISH

4 In a large heavy pot, heat 3 to 4 inches of vegetable oil to 365 degrees F.

5 With a sharp knife, make 3 shallow slits on each side of fish (to avoid curling).

6 Dredge fish in flour and shake to remove excess.

7 Fry until golden brown and crispy, about 5 to 6 minutes per side.

8 Pour sauce over fried snapper.

9 Garnish with basil leaves and scallion.

10 Serve with rice.

enchilado de langostino
Guantanamera, Cuban, courtesy of Arnoldo Gonzalez

Strictly speaking, *prawns* and *large shrimp* differ slightly in the shape of the heads, but the two terms are generally interchangeable, depending on which area of the world one is in.

SERVES 4

1 pound prawns or large shrimp
3/4 cup olive oil
4 whole cloves garlic
3 large plum tomatoes, diced
2 green bell peppers, thinly sliced
2 red bell peppers, thinly sliced
1/2 cup white wine
1 bunch scallions, julienned
1/2 cup seafood stock
1 teaspoon crushed red pepper
Salt and pepper to taste
Chopped fresh parsley for garnish

1 Peel and devein the shrimp.

2 In a large heavy skillet, heat the oil over medium-high heat.

3 Reduce heat to medium and add the garlic, tomatoes and bell peppers.

4 Cook 4 to 5 minutes; add prawns and cook 3 to 4 minutes. (Do not overcook.)

5 Deglaze the pan with the wine.

6 Add the scallions, stock and red pepper and cook an additional 5 minutes.

7 Season with salt and pepper and sprinkle with parsley.

8 Serve immediately.

alligator with guacamole

Delta Grill, Louisiana Cuisine, courtesy of Ignacio Castillo

While not really seafood, alligator is placed in the category because it lives in water. Commonly farm-raised, it is sold frozen and can usually be ordered through your fishmonger or on the Internet. Naturally, here it is served with avocado—or "alligator pear"—as in Bayou country folklore, they are thought to be cousins because they share the same skin.

SERVES 6

ALLIGATOR
2 pounds alligator tail meat
2 quarts chicken stock
1 quart water

3 tablespoons butter
Salt and pepper to taste

GUACAMOLE
2 ripe tomatoes, finely diced
3 jalapeño peppers, finely chopped
2 medium red onions, finely chopped
4 cloves garlic, finely minced
1 bunch cilantro, chopped
Juice of 4 limes
5 ripe avocados, diced
Salt and pepper to taste

ALLIGATOR

1 In a large stockpot, boil alligator over medium-high heat in chicken stock and water for approximately 1 hour.

2 When done, the meat should be the consistency of cooked chicken (tender but not mushy).

3 While alligator cooks, prepare guacamole.

GUACAMOLE

4 In a nonreactive bowl, combine the first five ingredients.

5 Add lime juice and avocado and toss.

6 Add salt and pepper to taste. Set aside and continue with alligator.

TO FINISH THE DISH

7 When the alligator is cooked, remove from pot and cut into $1^1/_2$-inch cubes.

8 In a large skillet, heat the butter until foamy. Add alligator and sauté for 3 to 4 minutes.

9 Season with salt and pepper.

10 Plate and serve with guacamole.

roasted fillet of striped bass with charmoula

Tagine Dining Gallery, Moroccan, courtesy of Hamid Idrissi

Also known as rockfish, this striped bass is given extra zing by the addition of charmoula. A Moroccan blend of herbs and spices, charmoula's intense flavor adapts itself well to many dishes, including chicken and vegetables.

SERVES 4

4 (6-ounce) fillets striped bass* with skin
1/2 cup Charmoula (recipe follows)
Sea salt to taste
1/2 cup pitted black olives, soaked in water to remove excess salt
2 lemons, thinly sliced

* Substitute any firm-fleshed whitefish for the bass.

CHARMOULA (Makes 1 cup)
1 large bunch cilantro
1 large bunch flat-leaf parsley
2 cloves garlic, peeled and crushed
1 teaspoon sweet paprika
1/2 teaspoon ground cumin
Juice of 1 lemon
2 tablespoons olive oil
Salt to taste

1 Rinse fish fillets and dry well with paper towels.

2 In a nonreactive bowl (stainless steel or glass), combine fish, salt and Charmoula. Gently toss to coat well.

3 Cover with plastic wrap and marinate at room temperature for 30 to 40 minutes. (Or marinate in refrigerator for 2 to 3 hours.)

4 Preheat oven to 500 degrees F.

5 Lightly grease a pan with olive oil.

6 Transfer fish to the pan and roast (skin side down) in the middle of oven for about 7 to 10 minutes.

7 Sprinkle with olives and serve with sliced lemons.

CHARMOULA

8 Wash and remove stems from the cilantro and parsley. Chop coarsely.

9 Combine all ingredients except olive oil and salt in a food processor and grind to a rough paste.

10 Transfer to a small mixing bowl and blend in the olive oil.

11 Add salt to taste.

NOTE: Charmoula can also be stirred into a pan of sautéed greens for an extra taste sensation.

tilapia asada

Guantanamera, Cuban, courtesy of Arnoldo Gonzalez

Found naturally from Egypt to South Africa and farm-raised worldwide, this sweet whitefish is believed to be the fish in the Bible's fishes and loaves story. In this Cuban preparation, it is marinated, roasted on a bed of vegetables and finished with a lapping of white wine sauce.

SERVES 4

MARINADE
4 whole cloves garlic, peeled
1/2 cup fresh lime juice
1 teaspoon dried oregano
1/2 teaspoon salt

4 (8-ounce) red tilapia fillets

SAUCE
2 cloves garlic
2 tablespoons fresh lime juice
1/2 bunch parsley, stems removed and finely chopped
3/4 cup olive oil
1/2 cup dry white wine
1 teaspoon ground cumin

VEGETABLES
2 Idaho potatoes, peeled and thinly sliced
1 medium onion, thinly sliced
1 medium green bell pepper, thinly sliced
12 green olives, pitted and sliced
2 bay leaves

2 hard-boiled eggs, quartered

MARINADE
1 Combine all ingredients and process in a food processor for 1 minute.

2 Place the fish fillets in a large baking dish and cover with marinade. Refrigerate for 2 hours.

SAUCE
3 Process the garlic and lime juice in a food processor for 1 minute.

4 Pour the sauce in a small bowl and fold in parsley, oil, wine and cumin. Set aside.

VEGETABLES AND FISH
5 Preheat oven to 400 degrees F.

6 In a roasting pan, layer the potatoes, onion, bell pepper and olives.

7 Remove fish from marinade and place over the vegetables. Discard marinade.

8 Pour sauce over fish and add bay leaves.

9 On the stovetop, bring to a boil over medium heat.

10 Remove from heat, place in preheated oven and bake for 18 to 20 minutes.

11 Garnish with eggs and serve immediately.

shrimp étouffée

Delta Grill, Louisiana Cuisine, courtesy of Ignacio Castillo

Étouffée means "smothered" in French. A Cajun/Creole roux uses oil in place of the butter used in French roux.

SERVES 4

ROUX

1/4 cup medium-dice onion
1/4 cup medium-dice celery
1/4 green bell pepper, medium dice
2 tablespoons Worcestershire sauce
1 tablespoon Delta Grill Cajun Seasoning Mix (see page 21)
1/2 cup vegetable oil
1/2 cup flour

ÉTOUFFÉE

3 cups chicken, seafood or vegetable stock
1/2 cup roux
1 tablespoon unsalted butter, divided
1/2 tablespoon chopped garlic
1/4 cup thinly sliced scallions
1 tablespoon Delta Grill Cajun Seasoning Mix (recipe follows)
1 1/4 pounds shrimp (16–20 count), peeled and deveined

2 cups cooked rice

ROUX

1 In a 2-quart stainless steel bowl, combine first 5 ingredients.

2 In a heavy skillet, heat oil until hot and smoky. Slowly add the flour while whisking constantly. Continue to whisk until oil and flour turn dark brown, being careful not to burn it.

3 Remove from heat and add to bowl with vegetables. Fold roux and vegetables together and set aside. (Extra roux can be frozen for future use.)

ÉTOUFFÉE

4 In a 4-quart stockpot, bring stock to a boil. Add the roux and cook on medium-high heat for 20 minutes. Sauce should have a gravy-like consistency. Strain into a bowl and set aside.

5 In a large skillet, add 1/2 tablespoon butter and heat until foamy.

6 Add garlic, scallions, seasoning mix and shrimp, and sauté for 3 minutes.

7 Add étouffée sauce and simmer for 4 minutes. (If sauce is too thick, add more stock.)

8 Add remaining 1/2 tablespoon butter.

9 Serve immediately with white rice.

moules poulette

Marseille, South of France, courtesy of Peter Larsen

Known as the "drink of the French cafes," *pastis* is the generic term for Pernod, Ricard and Pastis 51. This aniseed-scented liqueur, comprising 72 herbs and 6 spices, adds a unique flavor to this delectable mussel favorite from Marseille.

SERVES 4

2 tablespoons butter
1/4 cup finely diced shallots
1/4 cup finely diced leek
4 cloves garlic, thinly sliced
1 cup white vermouth
2 cups heavy cream
4 quarts mussels, beards removed and scrubbed
    clean
3 tablespoons pastis
3 ripe plum tomatoes, peeled, seeded and diced
    small
2 tablespoons minced parsley
8–10 basil leaves, torn into small pieces just
    before serving
Salt and pepper

French baguette

1 In an 8-quart stock pot, heat butter over medium-low heat. Add shallots, leek and garlic. Cover pot and sweat 3 to 4 minutes.

2 Add vermouth and reduce until almost dry.

3 Add heavy cream and reduce by half.

4 Add mussels, cover the pot and "steam" until they open. (Discard any that do not open.)

5 Remove mussels with a slotted spoon, leaving sauce in the pot.

6 Divide mussels among four heated bowls and keep warm.

7 Add the pastis and tomatoes to the pot and reduce sauce to the consistency of heavy cream.

8 Add the parsley and basil and cook for 30 seconds.

9 Season with salt and pepper and pour sauce over the mussels.

10 Serve with a generous amount of toasted French baguette.

sautéed skate wing with crispy fingerling potatoes

Le Madeleine, Modern French, courtesy of Fabian Pauta

A relative of the shark, skate is taken to its highest level when sautéed, dressed with classic French brown butter, and served with these oddly shaped but delicious potatoes.

SERVES 4

BROWN BUTTER
1/2 pound butter, softened
1/4 cup chopped black olives
1/4 cup chopped capers
Zest of 1 lemon
Zest of 1 orange
Salt and pepper to taste

FINGERLING POTATOES
8 jumbo fingerling potatoes, unpeeled

SKATE
4 (8-ounce) skate wings, skinned
Salt and pepper to taste
Flour for coating fish
2 tablespoons olive oil
Chopped fresh flat-leaf parsley

BROWN BUTTER

1 Blend butter, olives, capers, lemon and orange zest, and salt and pepper. Set aside.

FINGERLING POTATOES

2 Boil fingerling potatoes until they are nearly cooked. Place them in ice water to stop the cooking.

3 Slice the potatoes 2 inches thick. Set aside.

SKATE

4 Season the skate with salt and pepper and dredge in flour.

5 Heat the olive oil in a heavy skillet until very hot. Sauté the skate until crispy, 1 to 2 minutes on each side. Remove skate to a platter and keep warm in the oven.

6 Wipe out skillet and reduce to medium heat. Add potatoes and sauté until brown.

7 Plate fish and potatoes and drizzle with brown butter.

8 Garnish with fresh chopped flat-leaf parsley.

PASTA

Guess you can say I'm one of the new kids on the block. Originally from Egypt and doing international business, I was told that my thought to open a restaurant was not the greatest. Stubbornly, I clung to my dream, but wondered where to have it. In my search, I became intrigued with the history of Hell's Kitchen, its continued ethnic diversity and its future opportunities. I knew I had found the place and moved forward.

—George Youssef
36 West

spaghetti bolognese
à la josephine

Chez Josephine, French, courtesy of Richard Pimms

Jean-Claude Baker, son of the famous Folies Bergère dancer Josephine Baker, owns this romantic French restaurant. This classic meat sauce originating from Bologna, Italy, was a favorite of Josephine Baker and is a favorite at the restaurant too. Bolognese sauce can be prepared in quantity and frozen for a quick, delicious future dinner.

SERVES 4

¹/₄ cup extra virgin olive oil
¹/₄ cup minced onion
¹/₄ cup minced celery
¹/₄ cup minced shallots
¹/₄ cup minced carrot

2 teaspoons garlic
5 ounces ground beef
5 ounces ground veal
5 ounces ground spicy Italian sausage

1 tablespoon tomato paste
1 cup dry red wine
2 cups brown veal stock*
¹/₈ teaspoon ground nutmeg
¹/₈ teaspoon ground chili flakes
Salt and pepper to taste

1 pound spaghetti

¹/₂ cup freshly grated Parmesan
3 tablespoons chopped flat-leaf parsley

* Rich chicken stock can be substituted for the veal stock.

1 In a heavy Dutch oven over medium heat, heat the olive oil. Add onions, celery, shallots and carrots and cook until tender, stirring frequently.

2 Add garlic, beef, veal and sausage and cook thoroughly, until no longer pink.

3 Drain fat. Add tomato paste and stir 1 to 2 minutes to blend.

4 Add red wine and stock and simmer 15 to 20 minutes.

5 Season with nutmeg, chili flakes, and salt and pepper.

6 Cook spaghetti according to package directions. Drain and add to sauce. Stir 1 to 2 minutes to blend well.

7 Plate pasta and garnish with Parmesan cheese and parsley.

CHEZ JOSEPHINE

Located on 42nd Street on Theater Row, Chez Josephine's is a tribute to Josephine Baker, who made her name in 1930s Paris. Opened by one of her many adopted children, Jean-Claude, the restaurant was described in the *New York Times* as "the soul of Paris in the heart of New York." The colorful host, Jean-Claude, describes it as "a cocktail of human beings." Surrounded by Josephine's portraits and memorabilia, guests are transported to another era while dining on French bistro cuisine.

penne alla vodka
Mangia e Bevi, Italian, courtesy of Emmanuel Zitto

Penne translated from Italian is "quill pens." It is the ideal pasta to absorb the creamy tomato and vodka sauce, making this dish a favorite not only in Italy but around the world.

SERVES 4

1/4 cup olive oil
1 medium onion, finely chopped
2/3 cup vodka
3/4 cup canned tomato puree
1 cup heavy cream
Salt and pepper
1 pound penne pasta
3/4 cup Parmigiano-Reggiano cheese

MANGANARO'S HERO BOY

When asked what Manganaro's Hero Boy serves daily and at the annual Ninth Avenue International Food Festival, the immediate response is, "All that makes Ninth Avenue holy: baked ziti, lasagna, meatballs, spaghetti, and eggplant Parmigiana."

1 Heat oil in a large heavy skillet. Add onion and cook, stirring occasionally, until softened, about 4 to 5 minutes.

2 Stir in vodka and simmer for 4 to 5 minutes.

3 Blend in tomato puree and cream, stirring constantly for 4 to 5 minutes.

4 Season to taste with salt and pepper. Keep sauce warm over low heat, stirring occasionally to avoid sticking.

5 Cook pasta according to package directions. Reserve pasta water.

6 Add pasta to sauce and blend well. Toss in cheese.

7 If pasta is too dry, add a small amount of pasta water until it reaches desired consistency.

spinach fettuccine with grilled chicken

Druids, Irish, courtesy of Francisco Velazco

Having an affinity for butter and cream, fettuccine, also known as tagliatelle, is the perfect pasta with this velvety white wine cream sauce, while the grilled chicken becomes even moister with its brief simmering in the rich sauce.

SERVES 4

CHICKEN
4 (6–8 ounce) boneless, skinless chicken breasts
Olive oil
Salt and pepper

SAUCE
$1/4$ cup ($1/2$ stick) butter
4 cloves garlic, mashed and minced
1 shallot, finely chopped
12 ounces white mushrooms, sliced
$3/4$ cup white wine
$1^{1}/4$ cups heavy cream
2 tablespoons Parmesan cheese

1 pound spinach fettuccine

CHICKEN

1 Heat a stovetop grill pan over medium heat.

2 Brush chicken breasts with olive oil and season with salt and pepper.

3 Grill 4 to 5 minutes on each side, or until juices run clear.

4 Set aside and keep warm.

SAUCE

5 Heat butter in a heavy large skillet over medium-high heat.

6 Add garlic, shallot and mushrooms and sauté 4 to 5 minutes.

7 Add white wine and simmer 2 to 3 minutes.

8 Add cream and cook until sauce thickens and coats the back of a spoon, about 4 to 5 minutes.

9 Stir in Parmesan cheese.

10 Set aside and keep warm.

TO FINISH THE DISH

11 Cook fettuccine according to package directions.

12 Cut chicken breasts in 1-inch strips; add to mushroom/garlic sauce and heat over medium heat until sauce begins to bubble.

13 Serve over spinach fettuccine.

singapore mai fun

Mee Noodle, Chinese, courtesy of Harry Sim

This curried noodle stir-fry uses rice (*mai*) vermicelli (*fun*), and shrimp in this classic Chinese "pasta" dish.

SERVES 4

12 ounces mai fun (rice vermicelli)

1/4 cup chopped onion
3 tablespoons chopped green bell pepper
2 tablespoons chopped celery

2 tablespoons vegetable oil
1 egg
1/4 pound small shrimp, coarsely chopped
1 tablespoon curry powder (preferably Javin brand)
1 teaspoon salt
1 teaspoon sugar
1/4 cup chopped scallions

1 Soak rice vermicelli in cold water for one hour. Drain and allow to dry for 20 minutes.

2 Boil onion, bell pepper and celery for 30 seconds and drain.

3 Heat oil over medium-high heat in a wok, stir in egg, and cook 5 to 10 seconds.

4 Reduce heat; add vermicelli and stir-fry for 2 minutes.

5 Add shrimp and cooked vegetables; stir well and cook 1 to 2 minutes.

6 Add curry powder, salt, sugar and scallions, and stir well for 20 to 30 seconds.

7 Serve immediately.

butterfly pasta with baby peas

Barbetta, Italian, courtesy of Team De Cuisine

Its name meaning "butterfly" in Italian, farfalle is prepared here with both brilliant green blanched baby peas and sugar snap peas to create a springtime-fresh eating experience.

SERVES 4

2 tablespoons sweet butter
4 shallots, finely chopped
$1/2$ medium yellow onion, chopped
2 cups chicken stock
2 (10-ounce) boxes frozen tiny baby peas, divided
1 bunch Italian parsley, chopped
2 stems fresh basil, chopped
Salt and pepper to taste

12 whole sugar snap peas for garnish

1 pound Barilla farfalle pasta

1 In a large heavy saucepan, heat butter over medium-low heat. Add shallots and onion and sauté until they are soft, adding a little water as needed to prevent browning.

2 Pour in chicken stock, bring to a boil and boil for 5 minutes.

3 Add $1^1/2$ boxes frozen baby peas and boil an additional 5 minutes.

4 Remove peas from stock and place in a bowl of ice water to blanch (stop cooking and retain bright green color).

5 Let stock cool and place in a blender with the blanched baby peas.

6 Add the parsley and basil and puree. Season to taste with salt and pepper.

7 Boil the remaining 5 ounces of baby peas in water for 5 minutes. Drain and set aside.

8 Boil the sugar snap peas in water for 3 minutes; drain and set aside.

9 Cook farfalle in salted boiling water for 10 to 12 minutes, or until al dente.

10 In a large heavy skillet over low heat, combine pasta, puree and remaining whole baby peas, folding lightly. Heat through for 1 to 2 minutes.

11 Plate and garnish with sugar snap peas.

linguini with manila clams

West Bank Cafe, Progressive American, courtesy of Joe Marcus

Manila clams, originally from Japan, are cooked in a luscious dry vermouth and crème fraîche sauce, combined with pasta and topped with toasted bread crumbs.

SERVES 4

1¹/₂ pounds dried linguini

2 teaspoons canola oil
8 thin slices pancetta
2 teaspoons chopped garlic
1 tablespoon plus 1 teaspoon chopped shallots

4 dozen Manila clams
2 cups dry vermouth
³/₄ cup crème fraîche
2 teaspoons crushed red pepper

1 tablespoon plus 1 teaspoon parsley
1 tablespoon plus 1 teaspoon toasted bread crumbs

1 **In a large pot, cook pasta according to package directions.**

2 **In a large heavy pot, heat canola oil over low heat. Add pancetta and warm until the oils from the pancetta are released.**

3 **Add the garlic and shallots and turn heat to high.**

4 **Add the clams and vermouth and cook until the liquid is reduced by half, about 5 to 6 minutes.**

5 **Add the crème fraîche and red pepper and reduce until it reaches a sauce consistency.**

6 **Add the pasta and parsley and mix well.**

7 **Place on a large serving platter (family style) or divide into four individual pasta bowls.**

8 **Sprinkle with the toasted bread crumbs.**

theresa's sunday dinner
Mazzella's Market, Italian, courtesy of Theresa Mazzella

Theresa's Sunday dinner includes a variety of meats simmered in a rich tomato sauce and served over pasta.

SERVES 8–10

MEATBALLS
1 pound ground beef
1 cup bread crumbs
1 egg
$1/2$ cup Parmesan cheese
$1/4$ cup chopped parsley
Olive oil for frying

2 pounds boneless pork shoulder
2 pounds chuck beef roast, whole
2 tablespoons olive oil
1 pound Italian sausage links
1 large whole onion, chopped
2 (28-ounce) cans crushed tomatoes
2 (6-ounce) cans tomato paste
4 cloves garlic, minced
$1/2$ cup chopped fresh parsley
$1/2$ cup chopped fresh basil
Salt and pepper to taste

2 pounds dried ziti, cooked according to package directions

1 Thoroughly combine ground beef, bread crumbs, egg, cheese and parsley; form into $1^1/2$-inch balls.

2 In a large heavy Dutch oven, heat $1/4$ inch olive oil and brown meatballs in batches on all sides, about 10 minutes. Set aside.

3 Add more olive oil to the pot and brown the pork shoulder and beef roast separately; set aside.

4 Add 2 tablespoons olive oil to pot, heat and sauté sausage and onion until brown.

5 Return meatballs, browned pork and browned beef to pot.

6 Stir in the crushed tomatoes, tomato paste, garlic, parsley, basil, and salt and pepper.

7 Add 4–5 cups water and bring to a boil.

8 Reduce heat and simmer 3 to 4 hours.

9 Serve over cooked ziti.

bucatini all' amatriciana

Cascina Ristorante, Italian, courtesy of Gualtiero Carosi

Bucatini, a thick hollow spaghetti, soaks up an easy-to-make Italian sauce with the simplest and freshest ingredients in this popular Italian "working man's" supper. A salad and a loaf of crusty bread are the perfect companions to this dish, named after the town of Amatrice.

SERVES 4

2 tablespoons olive oil
1 large yellow onion, finely chopped
3 cloves garlic, chopped
1 cup pancetta (Italian ham), cut in $1/4$-inch dice
$1/2$ cup red wine
2 cups canned imported Italian tomatoes
   (chopped or pureed)
Salt and pepper to taste
Pinch sugar

$1^1/2$ pounds bucatini pasta

Basil leaves
$1/2$ cup grated Pecarino Romano cheese

1 **In a large heavy skillet, heat olive oil over medium-high heat. Add onion and garlic and sauté until golden brown.**

2 **Add the pancetta and sauté until brown.**

3 **Stir in the red wine and reduce completely.**

4 **Blend in the tomatoes and season with salt, pepper and sugar.**

5 **Over medium heat, continue to cook until sauce thickens.**

6 **Cook pasta according to package directions. Drain and fold into the sauce.**

7 **Garnish with basil leaves and sprinkle with cheese.**

8 **Serve immediately.**

braised lamb shanks with pappardelle

Le Madeleine, Modern French, courtesy of Fabian Pauta

Lamb shanks might be inexpensive, but they are one of the most flavorful meats when slowly braised with vegetables and fresh herbs and combined with sauce-absorbing inch-wide pappardelle noodles.

SERVES 4

LAMB SHANKS
2 large lamb shanks, 3 to 4 pounds total
Salt and pepper
3 tablespoons olive oil

1 small onion, sliced
1 carrot, sliced
5 white mushrooms, sliced
1 head garlic, unpeeled but broken into pieces
4 bay leaves
1/4 cup black peppercorns
1 sprig fresh rosemary
1 sprig fresh thyme

2 cups red wine
2 cups white wine
2 tablespoons tomato paste
3 tablespoons flour
Water to cover

PASTA
1 pound dried pappardelle pasta
2 tablespoons olive oil
1 clove garlic, peeled and chopped
1 tomato, diced
Reserved lamb meat
1/2 cup lamb reduction
2 handfuls baby arugula

GARNISH
Fresh rosemary or thyme

LAMB SHANKS

1 Preheat oven to 350 degrees F.

2 Season shanks with salt and pepper. Heat olive oil in a heavy Dutch oven and sauté lamb shanks. Remove lamb and set aside.

3 In the same Dutch oven, sauté the onions, carrots, and mushrooms for about 10 minutes.

4 Add garlic and spices and sauté for 2 minutes.

5 Add wines and tomato paste and cook until reduced by two thirds.

6 Over medium-high heat, whisk in flour and water and cook for 2 minutes.

7 Add lamb and cook in preheated oven for 2 1/2 hours.

8 Remove lamb shanks from sauce and remove meat from bones while warm.

9 Reduce sauce by half to make lamb reduction.

PASTA

10 Cook pasta according to package directions.

11 Heat olive oil in a large heavy skillet. Sauté garlic until lightly browned.

12 Add the tomato, lamb, lamb reduction, baby arugula and pasta.

13 Toss well and plate in pasta bowl.

GARNISH

14 Garnish with fresh rosemary or thyme.

pad thai

Olieng, Thai, courtesy of Nid Euashachai

This mainstay of Thailand is a delectable blend of exotic spices and diverse textures. It lends itself to variety, as the shrimp can be substituted with slices of chicken or pork.

SERVES 4

$^1/_4$ cup vegetable oil
1 tablespoon chopped garlic
1$^1/_2$ cups dry radish (also known as pickled radish)
$^1/_4$ cup extra-firm tofu, cubed
$^1/_4$ pound medium shrimp, peeled
1 egg, slightly beaten
2 cups rice noodles (soak in water for 15 minutes before use)
1 tablespoon sugar
1 tablespoon fish sauce
1 tablespoon tamarind juice
$^1/_4$ cup scallion, sliced
1 cup bean sprouts, trimmed, rinsed and dried
1$^1/_2$ tablespoons peanuts, finely chopped

$^1/_4$ cup raw bean sprouts, trimmed, rinsed and dried
1 lime, cut in wedges

1 In a large heavy skillet, heat oil over medium-high heat.

2 Add garlic, dry radish, tofu and shrimp; cook 3 to 4 minutes.

3 Stir in egg and scramble for one minute.

4 Add noodles, sugar, fish sauce and tamarind juice and heat through, about 2 minutes.

5 Add scallion, bean sprouts and peanuts and stir-fry 1 to 2 minutes.

6 Garnish with bean sprouts and lime wedges.

linguine alla vongole

Mangia e Bevi, Italian, courtesy of Emmanuel Zitto

Linguine, a long, narrow ribbon pasta, is Italian for "little tongues" and is cooked here with New Zealand clams (*vongole*) to create this classic Italian dish.

SERVES 4

³/₄ pound dried linguine
2 tablespoons olive oil
2 cloves garlic, minced
3 dozen New Zealand baby clams, scrubbed
1¹/₄ cups white wine
¹/₂ cup chicken stock
1 cup flat-leaf parsley, coarsely chopped
¹/₂ cup freshly grated Parmigiano-Reggiano
   cheese

1 In a large pot, cook linguine according to package directions.

2 While pasta cooks, heat a large heavy pot over high heat. When hot, add the olive oil and sauté garlic until lightly browned.

3 Add clams. When they begin to open, add the wine and stock and bring to a boil.

4 Boil for 2 minutes, and then cover and cook until clams open, about 5 minutes.

5 Discard any clams that do not open.

6 Drain al dente pasta and add to the pot with the clams. Toss well.

7 Cook over medium heat for 1 to 2 minutes, until pasta absorbs some of the sauce.

8 Divide into four pasta bowls and sprinkle with parsley and cheese.

9 Serve immediately.

Yes, the Holland has seen a lot and could tell a million stories. I've been here long enough to witness most of it.

I suppose one of my favorite times—back when HK was full of starving artists—was in 1952 when Paul Newman and Peter Falk would come in to play pool. A lot of times, Peter would sleep on the pool table. One of us would throw a blanket over him and leave him alone until the next morning. It was all very uncomplicated.

—Raymond Lentini
Holland Bar

truffle mac and cheese

West Bank Cafe, Progressive American, courtesy of
Joe Marcus

Toasted orzo with three cheeses is taken
to a new level with truffle oil and makes
this the ultimate French-influenced "comfort" food.

SERVES 4–6

24 ounces (1^1/$_2$ pounds) dried orzo pasta
12 ounces fontina cheese, grated
^{3}/$_4$ cup mascarpone cheese
4 scallions, medium chop
3 tablespoons grated Parmigiano-Reggiano
Salt to taste
4 tablespoons truffle oil
1^1/$_2$ tablespoons unsalted butter, softened

1 Preheat oven to 350 degrees F.

2 Toast the orzo in the oven until golden
brown, about 7 to 8 minutes.

3 In a large pot of boiling salted water,
cook the pasta 8 to 10 minutes, until al
dente. Drain, reserving about 1 cup of the
water.

4 In a saucepan, add fontina, mascarpone,
scallions, pasta and 1–2 tablespoons of
pasta water.

5 Cook over high heat, stirring constantly,
until the cheeses melt. If too dry, add a
small amount of pasta water.

6 Blend in Parmigiano-Reggiano cheese
and season with salt.

7 Remove from heat and fold in the truffle
oil and butter.

8 Serve immediately.

ARTISANAL CHEESE CAVES

Founded in 2003 by Chef Terrance Brennan,
Artisanal Cheese is the only facility of its kind
in this country. Cheeses are imported from
around the world and aged to perfection
under the most ideal conditions. The artisanal
cheese caves consist of five custom-made
caves designed to control temperature and
humidity to ^{1}/$_{10}$ of a degree. Cheeses age at
different rates and temperatures. The five
caves are divided into goat, blue, washed
rind, bloomy rind and tome. Also, wine and
cheese pairing classes held in the facility's
tasting room draw hundreds of participants
each year.

mofongo solo

Old San Juan, Puerto Rican/Argentinean, courtesy of
Victor Rodriguez

A tropical staple, mashed plantains are cousins of the banana but cannot be eaten raw. This Puerto Rican dish is served "alone," but precooked chicken, pork or shrimp can be folded in. It can also be topped with your favorite tomato sauce.

SERVES 4

3 plantains, very green
4 cups water
1 teaspoon salt
Vegetable oil for deep-frying (375 degrees F)

1 tablespoon olive oil, divided
3 cloves garlic, mashed and minced, divided
1/2 cup hot chicken stock

1 Peel the plantains and cut into 1-inch pieces.

2 In a bowl, add salt to water and stir to dissolve.

3 Place plantains in the water and let stand for 20 minutes. Drain well and pat dry.

4 Heat vegetable oil in a heavy, deep skillet or a deep fryer. Fry plantains about 8 to 10 minutes, being careful not to overcook. Drain on paper towels.

5 Using a mortar and pestle, mash 7–8 plantain pieces in batches with a little olive oil and a little garlic.

6 Spoon mixture into 4 balls. Flatten slightly and pour stock over them.

7 Serve alone or as suggested in introductory note.

turkish green beans

Troy Turkish Grill, Turkish, courtesy of Nurettin Kirbiyic

Used as a side, or meze, this Turkish favorite is easy to make and combines the freshest vegetables for a delicious and healthy dish. Because it is served at room temperature, it is a great make-ahead dish.

SERVES 4

2 tablespoons plus $1/2$ cup olive oil, divided
1 large onion, chopped
2 cloves garlic, finely chopped
1 pound green beans, trimmed and cut into 3-inch pieces
2 medium tomatoes, seeded and coarsely chopped
1 cup warm water
Salt and pepper to taste

2 tablespoons chopped flat-leaf parsley

1 In a large heavy skillet, heat 2 tablespoons olive oil over high heat.

2 Add onion and garlic and sauté for 2 to 3 minutes.

3 Add green beans, tomatoes and remaining $1/2$ cup oil. Lower heat to medium; cover and cook 10 to 12 minutes.

4 Stir and add 1 cup warm water.

5 Cover, lower heat and simmer an additional 3 to 4 minutes, until beans are tender.

6 Check occasionally and add a small amount of water if mixture becomes dry.

7 Season with salt and pepper to taste.

8 Cool and serve at room temperature.

9 Garnish with parsley.

tahini-dressed cauliflower

Gazala Place, Druze, courtesy of Gazala Halabi

Deep-fried cauliflower florets are tossed with the delectable Middle Eastern sesame seed paste mixture tahini. This dish can also be served as an appetizer.

SERVES 4

1 head cauliflower
Vegetable oil for deep frying

2 cups water
1 cup tahini
Fresh lemon juice to taste
Salt and pepper to taste

2 tablespoons olive oil
2 cloves garlic, minced
1 small onion, chopped

1 Wash cauliflower and cut into florets and set aside.

2 In a large heavy pot, heat 2–3 inches vegetable oil over high heat to 365 degrees F.

3 Fry cauliflower in batches until light golden. Drain on paper towels and keep warm.

4 Thoroughly blend the water, tahini, lemon juice, and salt and pepper; set aside.

5 In a large heavy pot, heat 2 tablespoons olive oil over medium-high heat. Add garlic and onion and cook 3 to 4 minutes, stirring constantly.

6 Add the tahini mixture, stir well, and gently fold in cauliflower to thoroughly coat the florets. Over medium-low heat, cook 4 to 5 minutes until hot.

briam

Uncle Nick's Greek Cuisine, Greek, courtesy of Antonio Manatakis

A classic Greek vegetable dish, briam is served as a side with grilled meat or poultry and can be served hot or at room temperature.

SERVES 6

3 pounds zucchini, cut into 1^1/$_2$-inch pieces
4 medium baking potatoes, peeled and cut into 1^1/$_2$-inch pieces
2 pounds ripe tomatoes, coarsely chopped
2 medium onions, sliced
3–4 cloves garlic, thinly sliced
^{1}/$_2$ cup chopped parsley
^{1}/$_2$ cup V-8 juice
^{1}/$_2$ cup olive oil
Salt and pepper to taste

1 Preheat oven to 350 degrees F.

2 In a large baking dish, combine all ingredients and mix well.

3 Cover and bake for 40 minutes.

4 Uncover and continue to cook for 15 minutes. Casserole is done when potatoes are fork tender.

5 This dish can also be served as a main course with bread and feta cheese.

eggplant charmoula

Tagine Dining Gallery, Moroccan, courtesy of Hamid Idrissi

Moroccan charmoula can be used as a vinaigrette or sauce in a limitless number of dishes: poultry, fish and meats. Here it is folded into eggplant, heightening the flavor of the vegetable, which can be served as a meze as well as a side.

SERVES 4–6

3 pounds eggplant
1/4–1/2 cup Charmoula (see page 148)
Olive oil for drizzling

1 Preheat oven to 425 degrees F.

2 Pierce the eggplants in several places with a sharp paring knife.

3 Wrap each eggplant separately in aluminum foil and place on a baking sheet.

4 Bake for 40 to 45 minutes, until soft. (A knife should go through eggplants easily when done.)

5 Remove aluminum foil and set eggplants aside to cool.

6 Cut eggplants in half and, with a spoon, carefully scoop out the seeds and discard.

7 Scrape the flesh into a large bowl and discard the skin.

8 Chop the eggplant flesh and blend in Charmoula gradually until desired taste is reached.

9 Place in a serving bowl, drizzle with olive oil and serve at room temperature.

braise of black-eyed peas and greens

B. Smith, Global Eclectic, courtesy of B. Smith

"Lucky" black-eyed peas and greens are flavored with barbecued rib meat and seasonings in this mouthwatering southern "soul food" side dish.

SERVES 6

2 tablespoons olive oil
4 cloves garlic, minced
1 cup diced sweet onion
1 cup diced celery
$1/2$ cup diced carrots
2 bay leaves
$1^1/2$ cups chopped kale or collard greens, stems discarded
1 cup diced pork, black forest ham, or smoked turkey breast
6 cups chicken stock
2 (15.5-ounce) cans cooked black-eyed peas, drained and rinsed
$1/2$ teaspoon Creole seasoning
$1/4$ teaspoon dried oregano
Sea salt to taste
Freshly ground black pepper to taste
1 cup cooked barbecued rib meat, shaved off the bone and chopped

1 In a large Dutch oven or saucepan, over medium heat, add oil and sauté the garlic, onion, celery and carrots until tender.

2 Add the bay leaves, greens and meat. Sauté, stirring, for 2 to 3 minutes longer.

3 Add chicken stock, black-eyed peas, Creole seasoning, oregano, salt and pepper to taste.

4 Reduce heat to low, add barbecued rib meat, cover and simmer for 45 minutes to 1 hour, until greens are tender.

5 Taste and adjust seasonings as needed.

arroz con azafron

Cafe Andalucia, Spanish Tapas, courtesy of Guillermo Vidal

Saffron, from dried crocus stigmas, is used to give brilliant color and unique flavor to this Spanish rice. While it is expensive, only a very small amount of the spice is needed to achieve the desired effect.

SERVES 4

3 tablespoons olive oil
1/2 cup chopped yellow onion
1/4 cup chopped celery
3–4 cloves garlic, minced
2 cups long-grain rice
Salt and pepper to taste
3 cups chicken or vegetable stock
1 teaspoon saffron
1/2 cup chopped cilantro

1 Heat oil over medium heat in a large saucepan.

2 Add onion, celery, garlic and rice, and cook until vegetables are translucent and rice is shiny, 3 to 4 minutes.

3 Season with salt and pepper.

4 Add chicken stock and saffron; bring to a boil and cover.

5 Reduce heat to medium-low and cook until liquid is absorbed, 15 to 20 minutes.

6 Fold in cilantro and serve.

almond rice pilaf

Landmark Tavern, Irish, courtesy of Francisco Velazco

Cooking the rice in chicken or vegetable stock heightens the flavor of this versatile dish. Easy to make, the pilaf is a great side for beef, chicken or seafood.

SERVES 4–6

2 tablespoons olive oil
2 tablespoons butter
1 small onion, finely chopped
1 cup Uncle Ben's converted rice
2 cups chicken or vegetable stock
$1/2$ teaspoon salt

$1/2$ cup sliced raw almonds, toasted
Salt and pepper to taste

2 tablespoons coarsely chopped parsley

1 In a large heavy saucepan, heat olive oil and butter over medium-low heat.

2 Add onion and sweat for about 5 to 6 minutes.

3 Add rice and coat well with onion mixture.

4 Stir in stock and salt and bring to a boil.

5 Stir, cover, and cook over low heat until liquid is absorbed and rice is tender, about 16 to 17 minutes.

6 Fold in toasted almonds and season with salt and pepper to taste.

7 Garnish with parsley.

portobellos in white wine sauce

Cafe Andalucia, Spanish Tapas, courtesy of Guillermo Vidal

These firm, meaty and robust mushrooms are actually cremini mushrooms that have matured a few extra days. They are sometimes referred to as the "thatched roof" mushroom.

SERVES 4

3 tablespoons olive oil
1 cup coarsely chopped yellow onion
2 cloves garlic, finely chopped
1 pound Portobello mushrooms, sliced in 1/2-inch strips
$1/2$ cup white wine
2 tablespoons soy sauce
Salt and pepper to taste

GARNISH
Scallions, thinly sliced OR
Fresh rosemary, finely chopped

1 Heat oil in a heavy skillet.

2 Sauté onion and garlic on medium-high heat for 2 to 3 minutes.

3 Add mushrooms and sauté until juices begin to evaporate.

4 Add wine and soy sauce; lower heat and cook for 1 to 2 minutes.

5 Season with salt and pepper.

6 Garnish with scallions or rosemary.

shrimp-and-ham-fried rice

Mee Noodle, Chinese, courtesy of Harry Sim

The egg in this stir-fry plays an important role, as it absorbs the oil and prevents ingredients from sticking to the wok. The combination of seafood, meat and poultry flavor adds delicious complexity to this Chinese dish.

SERVES 4

2 tablespoons vegetable oil
1 egg
1/4 cup chopped onion
1/4 pound small shrimp, deveined and cooked
1/4 cup ham cut in 1/4-inch dice
2 cups cooked white rice
1 teaspoon chicken-flavored bouillon powder
1/2 teaspoon salt

1 Heat oil in a wok or large heavy skillet.

2 Add egg and stir briefly for 30 seconds.

3 Add onion, stir well and cook for 2 minutes.

4 Add shrimp and ham and stir-fry for 1 minute.

5 Stir in the rice and heat for 2 minutes.

6 Season with bouillon powder and salt.

polentina

Becco, Italian, courtesy of Bill Gallagher

"Instant" cornmeal mush takes the work out of the Italian classic. Butter and fresh Parmigiano-Reggiano cheese unite to add richness to this "peasant" comfort food.

SERVES 6

2 quarts water, divided
2 fresh or dried bay leaves
1 tablespoon coarse salt, or as needed
2 tablespoons extra virgin olive oil
1$1/2$ cups instant polenta
4 tablespoons unsalted butter
$1/4$ cup freshly grated Parmigiano-Reggiano cheese

1 Boil 4 cups water in a 2$1/2$-quart saucepan. Lower heat to very low and keep warm.

2 In a 3- to 4-quart heavy saucepan, bring 1 quart water to a boil. Add bay leaves, salt and olive oil.

3 Working with a small handful of polenta, let it fall through your fingers into the seasoned boiling water while stirring constantly with a wooden spoon. Pay special attention to the sides and bottom of the pot as you stir to prevent sticking or scorching. It should take about 5 minutes to add all of the polenta.

4 When all the polenta has been added, the mixture should be smooth and thick.

5 Lower the heat and allow the polenta to bubble slowly. Cook, stirring occasionally, until it is smooth and shiny, about 5 minutes. If polenta becomes too thick, add water from the simmering pot, about $1/2$ cup at a time.

6 Continue to add $1/2$ cup water as needed until polenta is tender. (You might not need all of the reserved water.)

7 Remove saucepan from the heat, remove bay leaves, and stir in the butter and cheese.

8 Pour into a ceramic serving bowl. Let polenta stand about 10 minutes before serving.

9 The longer the polenta stands, the firmer the texture will be.

gomen wat

Queen of Sheba, Ethiopian, courtesy of Philipos Mengistu

Finely chopped collard greens are cooked in their own steam with mild seasonings in this Ethiopian vegetable dish.

SERVES 4

1 pound collard greens
1 cup olive oil
1 medium onion, finely minced
1 teaspoon finely minced garlic
$1/2$ teaspoon finely minced gingerroot
Salt and pepper to taste

1 Thoroughly wash the collard greens in a sink full of water and drain.

2 Cut off and discard the coarse part of the greens and chop the leaves and stems into 1-inch pieces. Set aside.

3 In a heavy pot, heat the oil and cook onion until soft and transparent.

4 Add garlic and gingerroot and simmer for 10 minutes.

5 Add the collard greens and stir well. Reduce the heat and cover until tender, adding a small amount of water if necessary to help tenderize the collard stems.

6 Season with salt and pepper.

mapo tofu

Mee Noodle, Chinese, courtesy of Harry Sim

Tofu and pork are stir-fried with a medley of seasonings in this quick and healthy Chinese dish. It is believed this dish was created by a pockmarked (*ma*) old woman (*po*) in her husband's restaurant.

SERVES 4

1 (1-pound) block silken tofu
1 tablespoon vegetable oil
2 cloves garlic, minced
1/4 cup ground pork
1 cup chicken stock
2 tablespoons Har Har Hot Bean Sauce (paste)
1 tablespoon sugar
1 tablespoon soy sauce
2–3 dashes Whaa Chiao (Chinese pepper powder)
1 teaspoon cornstarch
1 tablespoon sesame oil
1/4 cup chopped scallion

1 Cut tofu into 1-inch cubes.

2 Boil tofu in 4 cups water for 3 minutes and drain.

3 Heat oil in wok or large heavy skillet and cook garlic for 1 to 2 minutes.

4 Add pork and stir-fry until no longer pink.

5 Stir in the tofu cubes, chicken stock, bean sauce, sugar, soy sauce and Whaa Chiao.

6 Simmer 5 to 6 minutes.

7 Stir in cornstarch, sesame oil and scallion and cook 1 to 2 minutes.

8 Serve immediately.

Ingredients:
- 5 oz. fine sugar
- 2½ oz. flour
- 5 eggs

½ cup sug
1 cup m
1 table

6 oz Marg
6 oz Sugar
8 oz Porridge Oat

eggs whipping 1 - John Scots

¼ teaspoon baking Powder.

3 s sugar

flour. Almond essence
beat marg. & sugar together add
well then in flour + b. powder
spoonful in each tart
time 15 mins.

baking in and
bake in med.
oven for
15 mins

pinch of salt. Mix well together. Make
hole in the centre of the flour and pour in the
milk and water mixed with the egg (if used).
Mix well and form into dough. Break off
pieces about 4 inches long and nearly an
baking —

sure early delivery.
the Hoover is sold at
Hoover cleaner for
Vacuum cleaner,
than an ordinary
roughly.
teaspoon.

pommes à l'Alsacienne

an apple pie)
line a flan ring with tart or flan pastry, bak
cool. Half-fill with French pastry cream. Co
with overlapping close evenly sliced eat
apples. Brush with melted butter and bak
in a preheated hot oven (Gas 7, Mark 7)
for 5 minutes. Glaze with sieved apric
flavoured with a little rum spri

Bourdaloue
(Bourdaloue)

with tart or flan pastry, bake and
th French pastry cream.
fresh pineapple on this and
glaze. Serve chilled.

oue

poached pear halves.
French pastry cream.
ried macaroon
heated hot oven
utes. Serve chilled.

oz. of
1 of
arine
quickly
t into
s in a
en two
e them.

teaspoon.
a little
ave 10 mins
enough
doe.

My father, Sabastiano, purchased our two townhouses from the Astor family and opened our family restaurant in 1906. Yes, the Astors did build these historic elegant buildings in what is now known as Hell's Kitchen. I took over the restaurant 45 years ago and love continuing our family tradition of providing the elegance and refined dishes of Piedmonte to our guests. It truly has been a great century for our family!

—Laura Maioglio
Barbetta

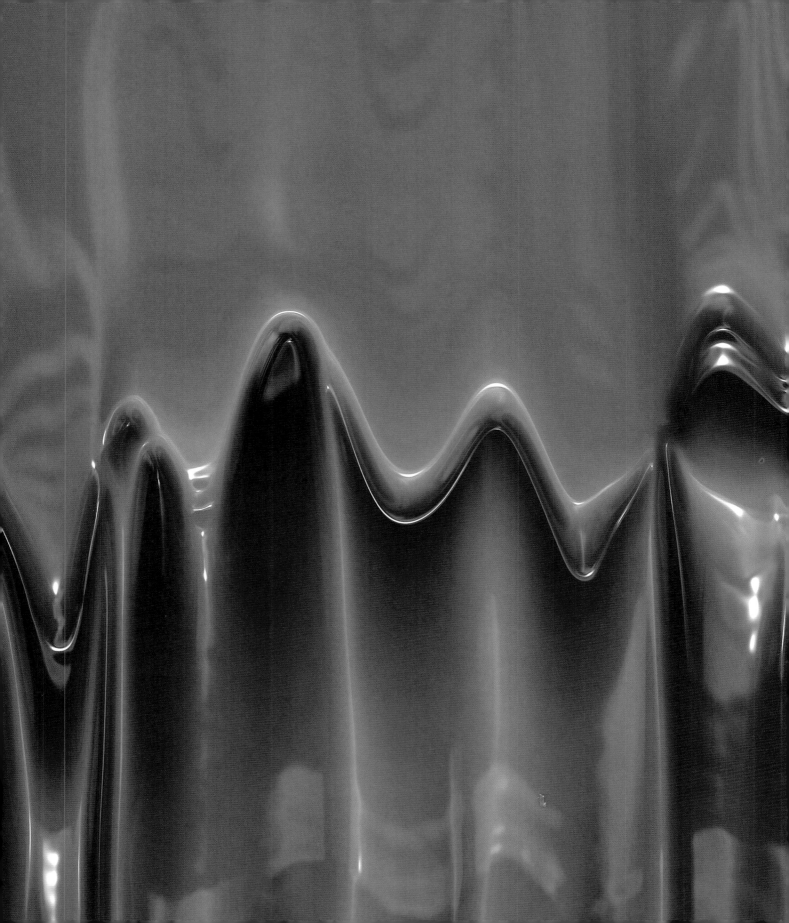

syrniki

Uncle Vanya Cafe, Russian, courtesy of Marina Troshina

Traditional Russian sweet patties are made with cottage cheese, flour and eggs and fried until crispy golden brown. Served warm with sour cream and cherry jam, syrniki is the perfect ending to a hearty Russian meal.

SERVES 4

1 cup cottage cheese
2 eggs, beaten
5 tablespoons all-purpose flour, plus extra for dusting
3 tablespoons sugar
2 drops vanilla extract
1/3 cup vegetable oil for frying

1 In a bowl, blend cottage cheese, eggs, flour, sugar and vanilla. Work into a soft dough.

2 Turn the dough onto a lightly floured work surface and roll into a 1-inch-thick log.

3 Slice the log into 8 pieces, coat lightly with flour and form into patties.

4 In a large heavy skillet, heat oil over medium heat.

5 Fry the syrniki in the hot oil until golden brown, 3 to 4 minutes each side.

6 Drain and serve.

south of the border sweet wraps

El Azteca, Mexican, courtesy of Maria Dias

Incredibly easy to make and delicious, these Mexican fried tortilla-wrapped bananas are best served hot, sprinkled with cinnamon sugar, drizzled with honey and topped with whipped cream.

SERVES 4–6

2 ripe bananas
12 (6-inch) flour tortillas
Vegetable oil

1 tablespoon sugar
1 tablespoon ground cinnamon
Honey to drizzle
Whipped cream

1 Cut each banana in half and then slice each piece lengthwise into 3 strips. (There will be 12 strips.)

2 Wrap each strip in a tortilla.

3 In a large heavy pot, heat 2–3 inches vegetable oil over high heat to 365 degrees F.

4 In batches, fry the banana wraps until golden brown, 3 to 4 minutes. Remove and drain.

5 Mix sugar and cinnamon and sprinkle over banana wraps.

6 Drizzle with honey and top with whipped cream.

tiramisu

Cascina Ristorante, Italian, courtesy of Gualtiero Carosi

A well-known Italian treat, tiramisu is the perfect "pick me up" frozen dessert, not only because of its richness but also because it is an easy make-ahead delight.

SERVES 6–8

2 cups espresso coffee
4 eggs, separated
4 tablespoons sugar
1 pound mascarpone cheese
2 (7-ounce) packages Savoiardi ladyfingers
2 tablespoons cocoa powder

RUNKEL'S CHOCOLATE FACTORY

A ninety-year-old lifetime Hell's Kitchen resident recalls her father and neighbors returning from work at Runkel's with their hair full of cocoa. Because there were only once-a-week baths at the public baths, she remembers her mother washing pillowcases on a scrub board to remove the cocoa. Retired at ninety-one, the now-deceased CEO of World's Finest Chocolate in Chicago, Edmond Opler, Sr., began selling Runkel's chocolate from a New York City pushcart in 1908.

1 Prepare coffee and set aside to cool.

2 In a large bowl, beat egg yolks and sugar with an electric mixer until thick and pale in color, about 2 to 3 minutes.

3 With a wooden spoon, gently mix in mascarpone cheese and blend until smooth.

4 In a separate clean bowl, beat egg whites until stiff. Gently fold into mascarpone mixture.

5 Quickly dip the ladyfingers in coffee and arrange half in a 9 x 13-inch baking pan (trim to fit snugly).

6 Spread half of the mascarpone mixture over ladyfingers.

7 Place another layer of coffee-dipped ladyfingers in the pan.

8 Spread the remaining mascarpone mixture on top.

9 Sprinkle with cocoa powder.

10 Place in the freezer for $1/2$ hour and then move to the refrigerator for 2 hours.

11 Cut into 6–8 square pieces.

torrejas

Guantanamera, Cuban, courtesy of Isaias Ortiz

The addition of Spanish port and sherry gives this "French toast" its Cuban twist.

SERVES 6–8

1 day-old French baguette, cut in 1-inch slices
1 cup milk
1 cup sugar
1/2 cup port
1/4 cup sherry
1 teaspoon ground cinnamon
Vegetable oil
4 medium eggs, beaten

SUGAR SYRUP
2 cups sugar
1 cup water
Zest of 1 lemon
Juice of 1/2 lemon
3 pieces star anise

GARNISH
Lemon zest

1 Spread the bread on a baking sheet and set aside.

2 In a bowl, combine the milk and sugar; spoon over each bread slice, being sure to soak each piece evenly.

3 Repeat procedure with the port and the sherry.

4 Sprinkle the bread with ground cinnamon and set aside for 10 minutes.

5 Coat the bottom of a large heavy skillet with vegetable oil over medium heat.

6 Dip each bread slice in egg and fry over medium heat until golden brown.

7 With a spatula, carefully turn slices and brown the other side.

8 Remove from skillet, set aside and bring to room temperature.

SUGAR SYRUP

9 Place all syrup ingredients in a heavy saucepan and bring to a boil over medium heat. Cook until sugar is completely dissolved, 2 to 3 minutes.

10 Remove from heat and cool to room temperature.

11 Pour the syrup over bread slices and refrigerate until chilled, 1 to 2 hours.

12 Serve warm or cold. To serve warm, reheat in a microwave.

GARNISH

13 Garnish with zest.

moroccan cigara

Tagine Dining Gallery, Moroccan, courtesy of Hamid Idrissi

This rich dessert combines typical Middle Eastern ingredients of dates, honey and almonds with a hint of orange blossom, all baked in a crispy phyllo dough. The perfect ending to a perfect meal is to serve these "cigars" with seasonal fresh fruit and a cup of strong Arabian coffee.

MAKES 10 "CIGARS"

1/2 cup chopped pitted dates
1/4 cup semisweet chocolate, melted
1 tablespoon butter, melted
1 tablespoon orange blossom water or 1 teaspoon orange extract
1/4 cup ground blanched almonds
1/4 cup vegetable oil (for moistening phyllo dough)
10 sheets phyllo dough
1 tablespoon honey
1 tablespoon sesame seeds

1 Preheat oven to 350 degrees F.

2 Combine first five ingredients in a large mixing bowl. Roll mixture into a thick paste.

3 Shape the paste into small "cigars" the size of an index finger.

4 Oil each phyllo sheet lightly. Place a "cigar" at the bottom of one sheet, leaving 1 inch from bottom edge and 2 inches from each side edge.

5 Roll from bottom edge containing mixture. Roll three-fourths up and then fold over side edges.

6 Continue to roll to end of sheets. Place cigars on an ungreased cookie sheet.

7 Bake for 10 minutes.

8 While hot, brush with honey and sprinkle with sesame seeds.

9 To serve, cut in half diagonally.

POSEIDON BAKERY

Founded in 1923 by John Demetrious Anagnostou, this Greek bakery is still owned and operated by his descendants. When John arrived in New York and saw the Hudson River, he decided to call his food establishment Poseidon, after the god of the sea. This shop is the last in Manhattan to make phyllo dough by hand.

red fruits soup

Barbetta, Italian, courtesy of Team de Cuisine

This unique Italian "soup" is a refreshing three-fruit dessert ideal all year-round, especially with the availability of frozen fruit.

SERVES 4

1 1/2 cups red wine
Juice from 1 lemon
2 tablespoons sugar
6 ounces frozen sour cherries, thawed
6 ounces fresh or frozen (thawed) raspberries
6 ounces fresh strawberries
2 tablespoons cold water
1 teaspoon arrowroot

1 In a large saucepan, combine wine, juice and sugar. Bring to a boil.

2 Add the fruits and bring to a boil again for 2 to 3 minutes.

3 In a small saucepan, heat water and arrowroot over medium heat until arrowroot is thoroughly dissolved, stirring constantly.

4 Pour over fruit and cook for 1 minute.

5 Remove from heat and cool before serving.

butterscotch toffee parfait

West Bank Cafe, Progressive American, courtesy of Joe Marcus

Using a popular candy, these parfaits are a snap to make but possess a richness that creates a wonderful dessert for everyday meals or an impressive dinner party. Gelatin sheets are available in baking and dessert shops and online.

SERVES 4–6

18 ounces Werther's hard toffee candy
1 quart heavy cream
3^1/$_2$ sheets gelatin
Fresh strawberries or raspberries

1 In a heavy saucepan, melt the candies in the heavy cream over medium heat, stirring constantly.

2 Plump the gelatin in ice-cold water, then add to the hot candy/cream mixture. Stir until all ingredients are well blended.

3 Pour into parfait glasses and chill. Garnish with berries before serving.

molten chocolate cake with smoked caramel

Zanzibar, African, courtesy of Raul Bravo

Little "volcano" cakes ooze rich chocolate from the center when pierced with a fork. While this delectable dessert could stand on its own, it rises to a more complex level when drizzled with a caramel and chipotle sauce.

MAKES 6 CAKES

CAKE

6 tablespoons butter
1 cup semisweet chocolate, chopped
2 1/2 teaspoons sugar
3 eggs plus 3 egg yolks
2 1/2 teaspoons flour
1/4 teaspoon salt

SMOKED CARAMEL

3/4 cup sugar
1 teaspoon chipotle peppers, finely diced
1/2 cup heavy cream
2 teaspoons butter, softened
1/4 teaspoon salt

CAKE

1 Preheat oven to 350 degrees F.

2 Butter and flour six ramekins and set aside.

3 Melt butter and chocolate in a double boiler.

4 Beat sugar, eggs and yolks together with a whisk until pale.

5 Add the chocolate mixture and mix until combined.

6 Slowly add the flour and salt and mix until smooth.

7 Pour into prepared ramekins and bake for about 12 to 15 minutes, until a wooden skewer inserted around the center ("volcano") comes out clean. After 12 minutes, check every minute to avoid overbaking. Center should be "molten" or gooey.

SMOKED CARAMEL

8 In a small saucepan over low heat, melt the sugar until golden brown, and then slowly add the chipotle peppers.

9 The mixture will harden, but continue stirring until the sugar dissolves again.

10 Once the sugar dissolves, add the cream, butter and salt; mix for 3 minutes more.

11 Remove from heat and blend in a blender or food processor until the mixture is a smooth consistency.

12 Unmold the cakes onto individual plates and drizzle the Smoked Caramel over the top. Serve with vanilla or chocolate ice cream.

arroz con leche

Guantanamera, Cuban, courtesy of Isaias Ortiz

Spanish-influenced Cuban rice puddings distinguish themselves with the flavors of lemon and cinnamon in an ever-popular worldwide dessert.

SERVES 4

$1/2$ cup long-grain rice, rinsed
2 cups water
$1/2$ teaspoon salt
Zest (strips) of 1 lemon
4 cinnamon sticks
1 (10-ounce) can evaporated milk
1 cup sugar
1 teaspoon vanilla extract

GARNISH
Ground cinnamon
Reserved cinnamon sticks

1 In a medium saucepan, combine the rice, water, salt, zest and cinnamon sticks. Cook over medium heat for about 15 minutes, until rice begins to split.

2 Add the milk and sugar and cook over very low heat, stirring constantly, until the mixture becomes creamy.

3 Discard the zest strips (rind) but reserve the cinnamon sticks.

4 Remove from heat and stir in vanilla.

5 Chill in individual serving cups or ramekins.

GARNISH

6 Dust with ground cinnamon and garnish with the reserved cinnamon sticks.

bananas with nutella and coconut sprinkles

Sortie, Belgian, courtesy of Akin Dawoku

Made in minutes, yet impressive, this Belgian dessert brings just three ingredients together to create a lovely blend of flavors. While the slices can be served alone, they are delicious served with warm crêpes and/or vanilla ice cream.

SERVES 4

3/4 cup Nutella
20 (1/2-inch) ripe banana slices
1/2 cup sweetened shredded coconut

1 **With a pastry bag, pipe 2 teaspoons of Nutella onto each banana slice.**

2 **Sprinkle with coconut and serve.**

bourbon street bread pudding

B. Smith, Global Eclectic, courtesy of B. Smith

The age-old question of what to do with day-old bread led to one of today's most popular desserts—bread pudding. While there are many variations on the same theme, this one not only adds kick with a Bourbon whiskey sauce but also gives tribute to New Orleans' world-famous street.

SERVES 6–8

BREAD PUDDING
1 teaspoon unsalted butter
3 large eggs
1 cup sugar
1/2 teaspoon ground cinnamon
1 teaspoon pure vanilla extract
1/4 cup raisins
2 cups heavy cream
8 cups brioche bread, cut into 1/2-inch cubes

BOURBON SAUCE
1/4 plus 1 tablespoon evaporated milk
1/2 cup sugar
2 tablespoons bourbon

GARNISH
Cinnamon
Powdered sugar
Whipped cream
6–8 strawberries

BREAD PUDDING

1 Grease a 6-cup loaf pan (8 x 8 x 2-inch Pyrex dish) with the butter.

2 Whisk together the eggs, sugar, cinnamon, vanilla and raisins in a large mixing bowl until very smooth.

3 Add cream and mix well.

4 Add bread and let the mixture sit for 30 minutes, stirring occasionally.

5 Preheat oven to 350 degrees F.

6 Pour the mixture into the prepared pan.

7 Bake for about 60 minutes, until the pudding is golden brown and set in the center.

8 Let cool for 5 minutes.

BOURBON SAUCE

9 In a heavy saucepan, boil the milk and sugar. Remove from heat and stir in bourbon.

10 To serve, cut pudding into serving pieces and drizzle with warm sauce.

GARNISH

11 Sprinkle each serving lightly with powdered sugar and cinnamon. Add a dollop of whipped cream and top with a strawberry.

arabian rice pudding
La Kabbr, Middle Eastern, courtesy of Farouk Mansoor

As with bread puddings, rice puddings are an international favorite. Basically sharing the same ingredients, they differ when accented with flavorings unique to the culture. In this Middle Eastern version, light, refreshing rosewater lends its special touch.

SERVES 6

1/2 cup long-grain rice
4 cups whole milk
1 cup water
1/2 cup sugar
1/2 teaspoon vanilla
1/2 teaspoon rosewater

GARNISH
1–1 1/2 tablespoons honey
1/4 cup coarsely chopped pistachios

1 Wash and soak rice in cold water for 30 minutes. After soaking, crush rice with a mallet.

2 In a large heavy saucepan, bring milk and water to a boil.

3 Reduce heat to medium; add rice and sugar. Cook, uncovered, for 30 to 40 minutes, stirring frequently, until rice is tender and pudding has thickened. Do not overcook.

4 Remove from heat and stir in vanilla and rosewater.

5 Pour into a serving bowl and refrigerate 1 to 2 hours.

GARNISH
6 Before serving, drizzle with honey and sprinkle with pistachios.

apricot and honey clafouti with toasted almonds

Marseille, South of France, courtesy of John Lee

A French country baked pudding, clafouti can be made with a variety of fresh fruits, including apples, plums and cherries. Let the season guide your choice. While it can be served cold, clafouti is best fresh from the oven while still light and airy.

SERVES 4

1/2 cup milk
1/2 cup heavy cream
4 eggs
1 teaspoon vanilla extract
Pinch flour
1/2 cup plus 1 tablespoon sugar, divided
2 tablespoons honey
1 tablespoon butter
6–8 apricots, sliced
1/4 cup sliced almonds, toasted

1 Preheat oven to 350 degrees F.

2 In a bowl, mix milk, cream and eggs and beat well.

3 Add vanilla extract, flour, 1/2 cup sugar and honey; blend well.

4 Lightly butter four individual ramekins and sprinkle with the remaining tablespoon of sugar.

5 Divide sliced apricots among ramekins and pour mixture over fruit.

6 Bake for 12 to 15 minutes, until set.

7 Remove from oven and top with almonds.

8 Can be served warm or cold, with lemon or vanilla ice cream.

THE HELL'S KITCHEN BEEHIVE

In 1977, a group of Hell's Kitchen residents noticed tomato plants struggling to survive in an abandoned lot. That was the beginning of the Clinton Community Garden, which continues to be maintained by volunteer residents. A highlight of the garden is the beehive populated with thousands of Italian Caucasian honeybees. Every fall, 80 to 100 pounds of Hell's Kitchen honey is harvested and sold to a lucky few.

tembleque coconut custard

Old San Juan, Puerto Rican/Argentinean, courtesy of Victor Rodriguez

Popular throughout the Caribbean, this easy-to-make coconut custard reflects the fresh tropical taste of the islands. Its name comes from the Spanish "to tremble," as it jiggles its way onto the plate.

SERVES 6

3 cups unsweetened coconut milk or 2
   (13.5-ounce) cans
$1/2$ cup sugar
$1/4$ cup cornstarch
Ground cinnamon for dusting

GARNISH
Fresh fruit
Mint sprigs

1 Blend all ingredients except cinnamon in a blender until well combined.

2 Transfer to a $2^{1/2}$-quart saucepan and bring to a boil over medium-high heat, stirring constantly.

3 Reduce heat to low and simmer custard until it coats the back of a spoon, about 4 minutes.

4 Pour the custard into six glass custard cups. Press a round of plastic wrap directly on top of each custard to prevent a skin from forming.

5 Refrigerate until firm, about 4 hours.

6 Unmold custards onto individual dessert plates and dust with cinnamon.

GARNISH

7 Can be served with fresh fruit and mint sprigs.

black and white chocolate mousse

Chez Josephine, courtesy of Richard Pimm, French

What could possibly be better than chocolate mousse? A double chocolate mousse—one white and the other black. It's the ultimate indulgence.

SERVES 4–6

DARK CHOCOLATE MOUSSE
1¼ cups heavy cream
4 ounces milk chocolate
3¼ ounces bittersweet chocolate
⅙ cup sugar
6 egg yolks

WHITE CHOCOLATE MOUSSE
¾ cup heavy cream, divided
7 ounces white chocolate
2 tablespoons sugar
1 egg plus 1 egg yolk, room temperature

GARNISH
Fresh strawberries or raspberries

DARK CHOCOLATE MOUSSE

1 In the bowl of an electric mixer, whip the 1¼ cups cream on medium speed until soft peaks can be formed. Transfer to another stainless steel bowl and refrigerate.

2 In a medium saucepan, bring 2 cups of water to a simmer. Place the chocolate in a stainless steel bowl on top of the simmering water and stir with a rubber spatula just until melted. Remove from the stove, keeping the bowl above the water.

3 Place the sugar and egg yolks in a medium-size bowl and mix with an electric mixer at high speed until double in volume, about 3 to 4 minutes.

4 Once the sugar mixture has doubled in volume, gently fold the mixture into the chocolate, folding from the center outward so as to not deflate the eggs. Continue folding until the mixture looks uniform.

5 Finally, fold the whipped cream into the mixture using the same technique mentioned above.

6 Cover the mousse with plastic wrap, allowing the wrap to adhere to the surface of the mousse. Refrigerate overnight.

WHITE CHOCOLATE MOUSSE

7 With an electric mixer, whip ½ cup cream on medium speed until soft peaks are formed. Transfer to a nonreactive bowl and refrigerate.

8 In a medium saucepan, bring 2 cups of water to a simmer. Place the chocolate in a stainless steel bowl on top of the simmering water and stir with a rubber spatula just until melted. Remove from the stove, keeping the bowl above the water.

9 In a small saucepan, bring the remaining 1/4 cup cream to a simmer. Once the cream has come to a simmer, add it to the melted chocolate and mix with a rubber spatula until it comes together and looks uniform. Set aside.

10 In a medium-size bowl, mix the sugar, egg and egg yolk together at high speed until double in volume, about 3 to 4 minutes. Once the sugar mixture has doubled in volume, gently fold the mixture into the chocolate, folding from the center outward so as to not deflate the eggs. Continue folding until the mixture looks uniform.

TO SERVE

11 Place 1 cooking spoon of dark chocolate mousse and 1 cooking spoon of white chocolate mousse side by side on each dessert plate.

GARNISH

12 Garnish with fresh berries.

METRIC CONVERSION CHART

LIQUID AND DRY MEASURES

U.S.	Canadian	Australian
1/4 teaspoon	1 mL	1 ml
1/2 teaspoon	2 mL	2 ml
1 teaspoon	5 mL	5 ml
1 tablespoon	15 mL	20 ml
1/4 cup	50 mL	60 ml
1/3 cup	75 mL	80 ml
1/2 cup	125 mL	125 ml
2/3 cup	150 mL	170 ml
3/4 cup	175 mL	190 ml
1 cup	250 mL	250 ml
1 quart	1 liter	1 litre

TEMPERATURE CONVERSION CHART

Fahrenheit	Celsius
250	120
275	140
300	150
325	160
350	180
375	190
400	200
425	220
450	230
475	240
500	260